Anyone can go to Heaven

Just be Good!

The path to Heaven and beyond to Nibbana

T Y Lee

Foreword by Ajahn Brahm

Basic Meditation by Piya Tan

Printed by : KepMedia International Pte Ltd
22 Jurong Port Road Tower A #04-01
Singapore 619114
Tel: 6896 0030 Fax: 6896 0070
Email: leeshin@kepmedia.com.sg

Book layout and cover design by : Geelyn Lim
Qzee Creations
geelyn@qzeedesign.com

CONTENTS

"The profound principles of the Buddha's teachings are systematically presented and lucidly explained by TY Lee in a very readable style that is contemporary, simple and convincing. A firm and 'friendly' stepping stone for seekers looking for an overview of the basic principles of Buddhism."

Venerable Aggacitta Bhikkhu
Sasanarakkha Buddhist Sanctuary
Malaysia

"Buddhism is more than a religion, it is a way of using the mind. Buddhists don't just have different beliefs from others, they gradually learn to use their minds differently and with the transformation of the mind everything else changes.
This little book offers a clear and easy-to-understand introduction to the Buddha's teachings. The reader will be challenged in some ways but inspired and encouraged in others. And those who take its message to heart will have the promise of a new, happy and fulfilled life."

Venerable Shravasti Dhammika
Buddha Dhamma Mandala Society
Singapore

Anyone can go to Heaven – Just be Good!

FOREWORD
by Ajahn Brahm

In 2005, I was told, the Swedish government sent a questionnaire to every high school student in the country. One question was "If you had to follow a religion, which religion would you choose?" Sixty percent answered Buddhism!

As Buddhism grows peacefully in our modern world, spreading only through reason and example, never by violence, there is an increasing demand for booklets such as this. Herein you will find the timeless wisdom of the Buddha presented with clarity, brevity and accuracy. Many often asked questions are directly and correctly answered. In all, this is a priceless little booklet to carry around, or share with your friends.

Truth ought to be simple. Kindness must be clear. And peace should be without complexity. This book is simple, clear and without complexity. I therefore recommend it.

Ajahn Brahm
Perth, Australia

Ajahn Brahm is the Abbot of Bodhinyana Monastery, Western Australia, Spiritual Director of the Buddhist Society of Western Australia, Spiritual Patron of the Buddhist Fellowship in Singapore.

PREFACE

I started this 'Just be Good ' project with the idea of having a few Buddhist promotional materials with a bright, positive and modern style. I later tied this in with a website offering more information on Buddhism for those interested to find out more. Little did I expect how popular the materials would become, and the effect of the website on so many people all over the world.

My aim is to present the basic concepts of Buddhism in a concise and down-to-earth manner, using an approach that many seem to find clear and accessible. The 'Just Be Good' project culminates in this booklet, based on the writings in the website.

For those reading this booklet without yet visiting the website, I would urge you to also go through the site. This is because it offers a further wealth of information by way of free e-books, talks on MP3 and links to other websites which provide deeper perspectives on many key points and areas.

I would like to thank with deepest gratitude Ajahn Brahm for giving me the courage and support to start this 'Just be Good' project, Ven. Dhammika for his patient guidance and advice throughout the project, Ven. Aggacitta and Ven. Kumaara for their many valuable suggestions and Sister Han Ah Yew and

Mr. Leong Kum Seng for their help in vetting the text. I would also like to express my most sincere appreciation to Bro. Piya Tan for writing the section on meditation for this booklet and Geelyn Lim for all her hard work on its design and layout.

Special thanks also go to all my teachers and friends in the Dhamma in Singapore for their encouragement from the very beginning. A big "thank you" and all my love also go to my parents and my wife, Susan. And my greatest appreciation is extended to the people all over the world who have given me the motivation and the strength to continue and develop this project. All mistakes, errors and omissions are mine alone.

May all Beings be well and happy, and free from physical and mental suffering. May all Beings embark on the Path of the Buddha and realize Nibbana. May all the merits of this project be dedicated to the happiness and emancipation of all Beings, and to help protect and spread the Teachings of the Buddha.

T Y Lee
www.justbegood.net

Diploma in Buddhism, Sri Lanka
Bachelor of Law (Hons), UK
Master of Business Administration, USA

INTRODUCTION

Interest in Buddhism is growing steadily worldwide, especially from people seeking answers in this current global age of clashing ideologies, fanatical strife and senseless violence.

Why is this interest growing so quickly, especially in the West? Perhaps it is because more and more people now realize that Buddhism is a Teaching that :

- **Emphasizes compassion, tolerance and moderation.**

- **Provides a clear path for spiritual and personal development.**

- **Has no room for blind faith or unthinking worship.**

- **Encourages questions and investigations into its own teachings.**

- **Teaches us to take full responsibility for all of our actions.**

- **Can be approached, realized and experienced, with immediate results.**

- **Says sincere followers of other faiths are also rewarded in the afterlife.**

- **Is very much in harmony with modern science.**

ANYONE Can Go To HEAVEN

ANYONE

What do we mean by ANYONE? Doesn't Buddhism say that only Buddhists are rewarded in the afterlife?

According to Buddhism, where we go to after this life **does not** depend on our religion. In fact, there is no requirement to pray to, worship, or even believe in the Buddha to have a good afterlife.

> What happens to us after this life depends on how we conduct ourselves in this present life.

> The path to Heaven is not by faith or worship, but by doing good and avoiding evil.

The Buddha never said anything like 'worship me and you shall be rewarded'. He also never threatened to punish anyone should they not believe in Him or follow His Teachings.

He said that there is nothing wrong in doubting or even questioning Him, as most people will take some time to understand His Teachings.

He stressed that everyone should seek, understand and experience the Truth for themselves, and not to have blind faith in anyone or anything.

Thus Christians, Hindus, Muslims, Jews, Buddhists, Taoists, and even atheists, are all able to enjoy a blessed afterlife. But of course provided, that they have been 'good' people!

HEAVEN

What do we mean by HEAVEN?

Heaven can be said to be a place where we can reborn in after we die. It can also be a state of mind.

For example, a hot-tempered person may constantly be in a bad mood and fly into a rage easily. Such a person will cause those around him, himself included, to be miserable and upset all the time. On the other hand, take someone who is even-tempered, with a tranquil mind and always at peace with himself and others.

Because of his state of mind, the hot-tempered person's life will seem like Hell to him and those around him. Needless to say, the even-tempered person, and those around him will enjoy blissful, Heaven-like lives.

The Buddha's Teachings allow us the experience of Heaven on earth by showing us how to attain such blissful states of mind.

Apart from states of mind, Buddhists believe there are several realms or planes of existence in the universe, and these can be places of suffering or places of happiness. Traditionally the realms of suffering, (or Lower realms), include that of Hell; and the Happy (or Higher) realms are the Human realm and the Heavenly realms.

Which realm or plane we will be reborn in depends on the kamma which we have accumulated for ourselves in this life, as well the kamma accumulated in our previous lives. This kamma is the result of our habitual acts and behaviour.

The size of the human population on earth is therefore not fixed or static as in a closed-cycle, as rebirth is not limited to only the Human realm. There are many other planes of existence in the universe apart from our own Human realm where we can be reborn in, or where rebirth can take place from.

If we end up in a Lower realm, will we be there for all eternity?

Buddhists believe that the length of time spent in a Lower realm will depend on the amount of negative kamma that has been accumulated.

There is no such thing as eternal suffering for anyone, no matter how much evil was done.

Even though it may take a very long time, suffering will come to an end once the negative kamma has been exhausted.

Thus Buddhism does not subscribe to any unjust concept of infinite punishment for finite wrongdoings.

Buddhism also does not 'threaten' the followers of other religions with any form of punishment whatsoever. Everyone has the freedom to choose different beliefs and paths for themselves.

Do we stay in a Heavenly realm forever? Is Heaven the ultimate goal?

Beings who have done much good and accumulated much positive kamma may be reborn in a Heavenly realm. If one is not yet able to achieve Nibbana, the Buddha encouraged all of us to lead upright and virtuous lives in order for us to be reborn in a Higher realm, and more importantly to protect ourselves from rebirth in a Lower realm.

While existence in a Heavenly realm may be for an extremely long time, it is still not forever. Beings in such realms will also eventually pass away and be reborn once their positive kamma has been exhausted.

As such, Buddhists do not consider rebirth in a Heavenly realm to be the ultimate goal. For most Buddhists, the ultimate objective would be to attain Nibbana.

It is said that Nanda, the Buddha's half-brother, was discontented and told the Buddha he wanted to give up the holy life. The Buddha then brought him to one of the Heavenly realms and showed him all its delights. The Buddha promised him that he would be able to enjoy all these delights if he practiced the Dhamma well. This inspired Nanda and he practiced very hard so that he could be reborn in that heavenly realm.

While practicing, Nanda gradually realized that Nibbana is a far greater happiness than being in Heaven, and he then released the Buddha from his earlier promise.

What then is Nibbana?

Without already practicing Buddhism and being on the path laid down by the Buddha, Nibbana can be a difficult concept to grasp or understand. It is like trying to explain colours to the blind, or sound to the deaf. Conventional language cannot adequately describe Nibbana. It has to be experienced to be understood.

However, in short, Nibbana is the total absence of all craving and suffering. It is achieved by one who has eradicated all aspects of greed, hatred and delusion. It is a state of permanent bliss and happiness from which there is no more rebirth.

The Buddha has taught us how to reduce, and eventually put an end to greed, hatred and delusion in all their various forms. And this can be done by cultivating the positive qualities of generosity and kindness, patience and compassion, morality and wisdom.

With the proper practice of Buddhism, it is thus possible for anyone of us to experience the peace and happiness of Nibbana, even in our present lives. Investigate, examine and try out the Teachings of the Buddha for yourself!

No need to wait for death,
experience Heaven while you are still alive.
Heaven right here and now,
is the taste of Nibbana in this very life.

JUST BE GOOD!

The Buddha's advice is to :

Do Good, Avoid Evil, and Purify the Mind.

In practical everyday terms, this means the practice of Dana, Sila and Bhavana.

What is Dana?

This simply means 'giving' or charity or helping others. This can be practiced in many different ways. You can do so through speech by using kind and encouraging words with others. Even giving something as simple as a smile can help another if it cheers them up and brightens their day.

You can always lend a hand to anyone who needs help. You can volunteer your efforts or your resources to the less fortunate. You can also share the Buddha's Teachings to anyone who is interested in them. It is the greatest gift of all.

However, try to do all this without regret, discrimination or ulterior motives. Practice Dana with kindness, compassion and empathy.

What is Sila?

This means 'Morality' and the Buddha advised us to observe the Five Precepts in the cultivation of Sila :

1. Abstain from killing any living beings.
2. Abstain from taking what is not given.
3. Abstain from sexual misconduct.
4. Abstain from lying and false speech.
5. Abstain from the abusive consumption of intoxicants and drugs.

These Precepts are not commandments but are rules that Buddhists take upon themselves to observe. They are observed not because of fear of punishment but because we realize that such actions harm others as well as ourselves.

For example, as we ourselves do not wish to be killed or harmed, we realize that all other beings also do not wish to be killed or harmed. Likewise as we do not wish to be victims of theft, adultery, lies and slander, we ourselves should avoid doing such acts to others.

The Buddha also strongly advocated avoiding intoxicants and drugs. This is because once you have come under the influence of alcohol or illicit drugs, you are capable of committing any acts that you would not have done otherwise.

Should you break the Precepts, the Buddhist way is to be fully aware that you have done so, try your best to make amends, and then resolve to try harder from then on.

Morality is the foundation which everything else rests upon. It thus might be good to memorize the Five Precepts so that you can be mindful of them at all times.

And once the observing of the Five Precepts becomes an instinctive part of your behaviour, developing its positive aspects will come easily and naturally :

1. The practice of Harmlessness and Compassion.
2. The practice of Kindness and Generosity.
3. The practice of Faithfulness and Responsibility.
4. The practice of Truthfulness and Pleasant Speech.
5. The practice of Self-control and Mindfulness.

What is Bhavana?

Bhavana means the practice of 'Mind Cultivation' or simply meditation. Meditation can be said to purify the mind by making it easier to develop Generosity and Compassion, and then to finally acquire Wisdom.

Buddhist meditation is usually classified into two types - Vipassana or Insight meditation, and Samatha or Concentration meditation. There are many forms of Samatha meditation, and Metta or Loving-Kindness meditation is one of its more widely practiced forms. All these types of meditation have their benefits.

However, it is usually recognized that it is through the practice of Vipassana or Insight meditation that we can come to fully know ourselves. And that through this we will be able to better realize and understand the Buddha's Teachings and to see things as they truly are.

Meditation can be said to be the highest form of Buddhist practice as the Buddha himself attained Enlightenment through meditation.

You do not need long meditation sessions to begin with. Even a short 10 to 20 minute session every day or every other day will do wonders.

Do we need to worship the Buddha, go to temples regularly, or make offerings or sacrifices?

Buddhists do not worship the Buddha. We consider Him as our Teacher and we thus respect Him as such. Buddhists bowing to a statue of the Buddha is simply our way of showing respect. This is akin to saluting a country's flag, or standing up while a national anthem is being played.

There is also no strict need to visit temples regularly. Many Buddhists however, do so to meet with fellow Buddhists or learn more about the Teachings. There is also no requirement at all to make offerings, and Buddhists certainly do not make any sacrifices whatsoever!

The Buddha said that the best way to respect Him is to practice what He had taught. This means a mindful and consistent practice, as opposed to visiting a temple once a week, and reverting to bad habits the rest of the time.

What is the significance of the Buddhist offerings?

Traditionally, joss sticks or incense, candles, and flowers are three of the common offerings. Informed Buddhists will know that these items are not really 'offerings', but are actually just symbolic reminders.

For example. joss sticks or incense remind us of the 'fragrance' of the Buddha's Teachings which pervade the world. Candles represent His Teachings which light our way in darkness. And flowers remind us that our lives are impermanent, like the flowers we 'offer'.

Flowers when in bloom are beautiful and sweet smelling, but will fade and whither after only a few days. Similarly, all of us will eventually grow old and die. Therefore, the flowers remind us that we should use as much of our time as possible to do good for others, and to practice the Buddha's Teachings.

So what basically is kamma?

Kamma literally means 'intentional action', and this refers to the Buddhist belief in the principle of Cause and Effect. We believe that every intentional act will give rise to a corresponding result, in either the present life or in a future one.

The results of kamma should thus not be seen as rewards or punishments for acts done, but simply the results or outcome of any such intentional acts. Positive actions will eventually result in positive consequences, and negative actions will eventually result in negative consequences.

Using an ordinary common-sense example of Cause and Effect, take a person who smokes, drinks and eats excessively without doing any regular exercise. As a result of his actions, this person will have a high likelihood of having a stroke or heart disease and ultimately go through much suffering. On the other hand, a person who watches his diet and takes good care of his body will usually be able to have a healthy life, even in old age.

Therefore, a person who has done much good and thus accumulated much positive kamma will likely enjoy a happy life and gravitate towards a Human, or even a Heavenly realm of existence in the next rebirth. Conversely, someone who has done many bad deeds and accumulated much negative kamma may have a life plagued with difficulties, and then also be reborn in a Lower realm of existence.

Kamma can also be viewed as seeds. You have the choice of the seeds you wish to grow. Therefore sow as many good seeds as you possibly can!

> **The importance of Kamma :**
>
> Kamma is the only possession we really own, and which we take with us from life to life.
>
> Every intentional act of body, speech and mind is like a seed planted; that will grow when conditions are right. Thus as you sow, you shall reap.

What if we have already done many bad things? Can we ask the Buddha to forgive us?

The Buddha is considered our Teacher and not someone that we pray to for forgiveness. Buddhists do not believe in any external agencies that we must ask forgiveness from, or worship for salvation.

If Buddhists were to ask for forgiveness, it would be to the person that we wronged, and not to a third party or external agency. If it were not possible to be forgiven by the person we wronged or to make amends, then we should let the matter go, learn from it and forgive ourselves, of course provided that we are sincere about it.

The Buddha teaches us that we are each responsible for our own actions, and that we are each capable of shaping our own destinies. We should thus consider carefully before doing anything wrong, and instead try to do right at all times.

If you are unsure whether an action is right or wrong, you can apply this simple rule of thumb as taught by the Buddha : if the action harms either yourself or another, or both; then avoid doing that action. If not, then go right on ahead!

Abraham Lincoln :
"When I do good, I feel good.
When I do bad, I feel bad.
That's my religion."

What then can we do to overcome the negative kamma from any bad deeds that we may have done?

According to the principle of Cause and Effect, negative kamma cannot simply be erased by positive kamma. Any act intentionally done will have its consequences in either the near or far future.

The Buddha used the analogy of salt in a river to advise us on how to diminish the effects of negative kamma. He said that while a tablespoon of salt will make a cup of water very salty, this same tablespoon of salt will have practically no effect on the taste of a river.

Simply put, dilute any negative kamma you may have by accumulating more positive kamma.

And positive kamma is accumulated by the practice of Dana, Sila and Bhavana.

The Buddha :
"Do not disregard merit saying it will not come to me.
By each drop of water is a water-jar filled.
Similarly the wise man gathering little by little,
fills himself with good."

BASIC BUDDHISM

The Buddha

Siddhattha Gotama was born into the family of a ruling clan about 2,500 years ago. His father was the chief of this clan which lived in northern India close to the border of what is now Nepal. As the only son of the chief, he lived a life of ease and luxury surrounded by riches and women. However, even as a youth he realized that he would get no lasting satisfaction from such a lifestyle.

He began to see that all human existence is unavoidably subject to illness, old age and death. At the age of 29, and inspired by the sight of a calm and dignified hermit, he decided to forgo his luxurious lifestyle. He left his wife and child in the good hands of the royal family to seek the answers to lasting happiness. After 6 years of wandering and severe ascetic practices, he realized that neither a decadent lifestyle nor extreme asceticism would lead him to the answers he sought.

He decided to pursue the 'Middle Way' between these two extremes. He then settled down under a Bodhi tree, relaxed, had a good meal and resolved not to get up until he found the answers. After a night of deep meditation, full understanding came to him. From then on, the Prince became known as the Buddha which means literally, the 'Awakened One'.

The Buddha then spent the next 45 years of His life teaching what He finally came to understand. He founded a community of monks known as the Sangha, and Buddhism spread throughout northern India. Kings, nobles, merchants and peasants became His disciples and followers, and even now countless people everywhere benefit from His Teachings.

He passed away peacefully into final Nibbana at the age of 80.

The Four Noble Truths

On gaining enlightenment, the Buddha realized the Four Noble Truths.

1. **All beings are subject to Dukkha.**
   Dukkha is usually translated as suffering but it actually encompasses a wide range of negative feelings including stress, dissatisfaction and physical suffering. Dukkha exists as all beings are subject to illness, separation from loved ones, not getting their desires, aging and death.

2. **Dukkha arises from desire and craving.**
   All beings crave pleasant sensations, and also desire to avoid unpleasant sensations. These sensations can be physical or psychological, and dukkha arises when these desires and cravings are not met.

3. **Dukkha can be overcome by the elimination of desire and craving.**
   Nibbana is the state of peace where all greed, hatred and delusion, and thereby dukkha, have been eradicated.

4. **There is a way out of dukkha, which is the Noble Eightfold Path.**
   Dukkha can be reduced, weakened and finally eradicated and Nibbana thereby attained, by following this path as taught by the Buddha.

Buddhism is occasionally criticized as being overly pessimistic as it seems to focus on suffering rather than on happiness and joy. However, all conditions of happiness and joy are impermanent because all beings are subject to sickness, old age and death, and as a result, all beings are undeniably subject to dukkha.

Instead, Buddhism is actually realistic as the Buddha has taught us how to overcome or reduce dukkha, and how to achieve the permanent bliss of Nibbana. By following the Noble Eightfold Path taught by the Buddha, Nibbana can be experienced even in this present lifetime.

The Noble Eightfold Path

1. **Right Understanding**
   To understand and accept the Four Noble Truths.

2. **Right Thought**
   To cultivate thoughts of generosity, loving-kindness and compassion.

3. **Right Speech**
   To refrain from lying, slander, harsh words and gossip. To cultivate truthful, peaceful, kind and meaningful speech.

4. **Right Action**
   To abstain from killing, stealing and sexual misconduct. To cultivate harmlessness, honesty and faithfulness.

5. **Right Livelihood**
   To avoid occupations involving killing (of both humans and animals), the sale of animal flesh, the trading of humans, weapons, poisons and intoxicants. Occupations which are unethical, immoral and illegal should also be avoided.

6. **Right Effort**
   To apply mental discipline to prevent unwholesome thoughts from arising, and to dispel unwholesome thoughts that have arisen. To develop wholesome thoughts, and to maintain those wholesome thoughts that have arisen.

7. **Right Mindfulness**
   To be aware of the body, and bodily postures and sensations. To be aware of the mind and its thoughts, emotions and feelings.

8. **Right Concentration**
   To practice meditation to train the mind to be focused and disciplined in order to cultivate and acquire wisdom.

The Three Marks of Existence

The Buddha also discovered that all existence has three characteristics.

Anicca
All things are impermanent, and everything is in the process of changing into something else. For example,

we are all in the process of aging. Even the stars and galaxies are in the process of change.

Dukkha

Because all things are impermanent, existence is subject to dukkha. There will always be the craving for the pleasant, and the aversion to the unpleasant, resulting from the ever-changing nature of existence.

Anatta

There is no permanent or unchanging self. The 'self' which we are conditioned to believe exists, is comprised of nothing more than different mental and physical constituents, which are in a state of constant change because of Cause and Effect.

Rebirth

Because there is no permanent unchanging self, Buddhism denies the existence of an unvarying immortal soul passing from one life to the next. According to Buddhism, the mind or consciousness moves from one life to the next.

In a seeming paradox, a 70 year old person is neither different from nor similar to, the person he was as a 20 year old. This difference and similarity is both psychological and physical. Likewise, the mind or consciousness which moves from one life to the next is also neither different from nor similar to that of the previous life. The Buddha also discovered that all existence has three characteristics.

For example, if the flame from a candle is used to light another candle, the flame of the second candle is neither the same nor different from that of the first candle. This is even though the flame from the second candle originated from the first candle.

Kamma is carried along with the consciousness towards the next life.

At first these may be difficult concepts to grasp. But with knowledge and understanding, and the practice of Insight meditation, realization and comprehension will eventually arise in the practitioner.

The Buddhist Texts

The Teachings of the Buddha, known also as the Dhamma, were collated into three separate sets of books. These books are collectively known as the Tipitaka, or the Three Baskets. The total amount of material is vast and is estimated to be more than twice that of the Encyclopaedia Britannica.

Although some changes and revisions in the Tipitaka are inevitable over the 2,500 years or so it has been in existence, it is estimated that up to 90% of the Teachings remain unaltered. This is because when it was recited, it was done so with several hundred monks reciting together at the same time. When it was finally committed to writing around 80 BC, large groups of monks also undertook this task in unison. This made changing or altering the Tipitaka very difficult. Reproductions of the original texts survive today and are well preserved in Sri Lanka.

The Sutta Pitaka
Subdivided into five separate collections, the Sutta Pitaka contains all of the Buddha's discourses as well as several from His most senior disciples. The Buddha was extremely successful in His Teachings as He used the language of the common people, which is called Pali.

He adapted the manner and style of His discourses such that He used simpler concepts for the ordinary folk, and more complex ideas for educated and intellectual audiences. He taught everyone from peasants to kings.

The Teachings range from guidelines for individual behaviour to highly sophisticated commentaries on politics and social philosophy. They are pragmatic and readily applicable to daily life. And despite being taught more than 2,500 years ago, His Teachings are still very much pertinent today.

The Vinaya Pitaka

Also divided into five books, the Vinaya Pitaka lays down the rules and guidelines for the Sangha or the community of monks and nuns. With every monk and nun having equal rights, the Sangha is possibly the earliest form of a democratically governed organization still functioning today.

The Abhidhamma Pitaka

Known as the Higher Teachings of the Buddha, the Abhidhamma Pitaka is a monumental and extremely complex and sophisticated approach to the Dhamma. It contains the Buddhist doctrines arranged and classified in a highly systematic set of seven books.

Although traditionally attributed to the Buddha, many commentators now regard the Abhidhamma as the work of later scholar monks who distilled the Teachings of the Buddha into this amazing set of documents.

It deals with the concepts of existence and reality. It analyzes the human thought processes and examines the constituents of mind and matter. Many of its concepts relating to reality and perception have anticipated the works of modern thinkers and scientists.

The Buddhist Traditions

Why are there different Buddhist traditions?

Buddhism was founded more than 2,500 years ago, and through this long passage of time, three main traditions have evolved. These developments took place as Buddhism adapted to the conditions and cultures of the different countries it spread to.

However, the Buddha's Teachings have proved to be very resilient as while the outer trappings may be dissimilar, the core Buddhist doctrines remain the same among the various traditions. For example, the acceptance of the core doctrines, or "Unifying Points", between the different traditions was formally endorsed by the World Buddhist Sangha Council in Sri Lanka in 1966.

Buddhists accept and respect diversity, and consider the various traditions merely as different routes to the same destination. Generally, the different traditions assist and support each other along this route.

Briefly, what are these different Buddhist traditions?

The Theravada tradition is the oldest and most conservative. It is the closest to the original form of Buddhism as taught by the Buddha Himself. It is simpler than the other traditions in approach, with few ceremonies and rituals, stressing instead on discipline and morality and the practice of meditation.

The Mahayana tradition started to develop in India between about 200 B.C. and 100 A.D. It has adapted to different Asian cultures absorbing elements of Hinduism and Taoism. Mahayana Buddhism emphasizes compassion and faith with the goal of helping all others attain enlightenment. The Zen, Nichiren and Pureland sects are included in Mahayana Buddhism.

The Vajrayana or Tibetan tradition arose in India around 700 A.D. when Buddhist Indian monks brought over to Tibet a brand of Buddhism with tantric practices. This combined with elements of the local Bon religion, gives Vajrayana some of its unique practices. It tends to rely more on rituals, mantra chanting and visualizations. The most well-known figure of Buddhism, the Dalai Lama, is the spiritual head of the Vajrayana tradition.

In Buddhism, the different traditions are viewed like different flavours of ice-cream. It is the same thing but with different tastes appealing to different people.

Why are the same words spelt differently in the various Buddhist traditions?

During the time of the Buddha, the language commonly used was Pali, as opposed to Sanskrit which was used primarily by the Brahmins, the priests of Hinduism. The Buddha chose to speak and teach mainly in Pali as He wanted as many people as possible to learn and benefit from His Teachings.

The Theravada school of Buddhism uses Pali spellings and pronunciations, and the Mahayana/Zen and Tibetan schools use mainly Sanskrit. Examples of Pali spellings would be Dhamma, kamma, nibbana. The Sanskrit versions of these words would be Dharma, karma, nirvana.

This booklet uses Pali spellings as Pali is the language closest to that used by the Buddha Himself.

MORE QUESTIONS...
AND ANSWERS

Kamma, rebirth, and the inequalities of life

Does kamma explain why there is so much inequality of life around us?

People have always wondered about the fairness of life, and why everyone is not born equal.

Questions are always asked about why is one person so healthy, and another born with many physical afflictions. Why is one person born into a very wealthy family, and another born into abject poverty. Why is one person able to enjoy a long and happy life, and another having their life cut short by violence or accident.

Buddhists do not believe that all these inequalities are because of chance, or the unexplainable will of an unseen and omnipotent heavenly being. We believe that kamma and the principle of Cause and Effect account for most of these differences in people's lives.

If we can't remember anything from our previous lives, is it then fair to suffer in this life for something done wrong in a previous life?

Keep in mind that kamma is not a system of rewards or punishments. It is simply a natural principle that any intentional act will have its corresponding result, when conditions are right.

Take for example a person who gets drunk, and then trips and falls into a ditch. He breaks his leg. That person may have no memory of falling and getting hurt, but he is still subject to the painful result of his actions.

As mentioned earlier, kamma can also be viewed like the planting of seeds. If you plant an apple seed, an apple tree will grow. If you plant an oak seed, an oak tree will grow. It is just the principle of Cause and Effect.

Thus, fairness and memory are not factors in kamma and this applies equally to all beings in existence.

If there is rebirth, why don't people remember their past lives?

Memories of past lives lie deep in the subconscious mind. We are usually unable to access these memories because our minds are not clear, or disciplined enough. For example, very few of us can recall what we did on the same day of even just a month ago! However, research has shown that some young children whose minds remain reasonably clear, may be able to spontaneously recall their past lives.

Western psychoanalysts are now using methods of hypnotic regression to help patients with psychological problems, and some of these patients seem to be able to recall their past lives under such therapy. Monks with highly disciplined minds and who are able to enter into deep meditative states are also said to be able to recall their past lives.

If we won't know anything about our next life, then why worry about it?

That would be a slightly selfish attitude to take. It would be similar to irresponsible parents who are going to spend everything they have without leaving anything for their children. They won't know for sure what is going to happen to their children either. Responsible parents will do everything they can to ensure the best for their offspring whether they will be around to see the results or not. We should take a similar approach for the being in our next life.

However, it is said in the Buddhist texts that some Heavenly beings, and also some beings reborn in the Lower realms are in fact able to recall their past lives. Some of these beings have described the deeds which resulted in the conditions of their rebirth. There is thus some incentive to do the best we can in this life.

In any case, as Buddhists we should do the best we can in this life, whether or not we will experience positive results in the next life.

There is a meaningful saying in Buddhism which bears some thinking about :

> **"If you want to know what kind of life you led in your past life, look at your present life.**
>
> **If you want to know what kind of life you will have in your next life, look at your present life."**

Is there any scientific proof of rebirth?

There are in fact many well researched and documented cases of people, including many children, who remember their past lives. While there are countless instances of anecdotal evidence from the East, studies in this area have also been done by many Western researchers.

This research was done on both Asian and Western subjects and took place under scientific conditions and with rigorous examinations. The conclusion reached is that not only is rebirth probable, it is just about as good as proven.

For example, Carol Bowman has written books on children who are able to recall their past lives. These are not religious or spiritual books, but are well-documented case studies based on the observation and empirical research done on hundreds of children.

Prof. Ian Stevenson was an eminent psychiatrist and director of The Division of Perceptual Studies at the University of Virginia in the USA. Prof. Stevenson's publications, which are meant primarily for the academic and scientific community, detail over 3,000 case studies of people who could remember their past lives.

Other well known and reputable researchers and authorities on this subject are Dr. Jim Tucker, Dr. Raymond Moody and Thomas Shroder.

Henry Ford :
"Work is useless if we cannot use our experience in
 another life."
"Genius is the fruit of long experience in many lives.
 Of this I am sure, we are here for a purpose.
 We will go on. Mind and memory, they are eternal."

Buddhism and modern science

Does Buddhism conflict with modern science?

Among all the major religions of the world, the Buddhist teachings
do not have any major or significant conflicts with the discoveries
of modern science. It does not have any creation myths, nor
does it attempt to attribute any natural phenomenon to
supernatural causes.

It embraces fully the Theory of Evolution which quite clearly
demonstrates the Buddhist doctrine of Impermanence. Thus, it
has no difficulties with fossil remains, carbon-dating and geological
evidence with which modern science uses to date the age of the
earth to be around 4.5 billion years. These discoveries in fact
confirm the Buddha's comment that the earth has been in
existence for eons.

The Buddha had said specifically that there are countless star
systems in existence, and that our world is like a speck of dust
compared to the vastness and diversity of the universe. He did
not claim that the earth was created by an unseen deity or that
humans are a special creation of that deity.

Using modern astronomy, satellites and radio telescopes, we can
observe the trillions of stars and billions of galaxies in the universe;

and see clearly that the Buddha made a very accurate observation of our place in the cosmos.

The Buddha's concept of time, in the context of the universe, seems to be very much in accordance with modern science. Buddhism measures the timescale of the universe in 'kalpas' which are inconceivably long periods of time. He gave the analogy of a silk cloth brushing the top of a mountain once every hundred years. The time it takes for the mountain to be worn away is approximately the duration of one 'kalpa'. Therefore Buddhist cosmology is quite in line with current scientific estimates of the age of the universe, which is taken to be about 13.7 billion years old.

Also very interestingly, The Buddha mentioned that the universe is in a continual state of expansion and contraction and that these cycles last for unimaginably long periods of time, or for many, many 'kalpas'. It seems that He anticipated the Oscillating Universe Theory by more than 2,500 years.

In one of His discourses, the Buddha held up a cup of water and said that there are countless living beings in the water. For a long time, nobody understood what He meant, but today we can see with a microscope that there are in fact numerous micro-organisms in any cup of water. Thus there may still be many things the Buddha said that we have yet to discover and comprehend.

William Shakespeare, in "Hamlet" :
"There are more things in heaven and earth, Horatio,
than are dreamt of in your philosophy."

Buddhism and creation myths

In Buddhism, why isn't there a belief in a supreme god that created the universe?

Buddhists tend to be fairly realistic in such matters and do not believe in creation myths such as the universe emerging from a cosmic egg, or created by an old man with a long, white beard. If anything we believe that the universe has always existed.

If it is said that an omnipotent being or 'intelligent designer' did create the universe, then it begs the obvious question of who then created or 'designed' that being? And if that being has always existed, then isn't it more believable that the universe has always been in existence instead?

In any case, Buddhists certainly don't believe in any such all-powerful and all-knowing being that, for whatever reasons, allows its creations to be tortured in an everlasting hell, (which that being also created). And if that omniscient being knows beforehand that most of its creations are destined to burn in hell forever, then why does it go ahead to produce so much suffering? It is hard also for Buddhists to believe in such a supreme being that somehow manages to be loving and forgiving, while at the same time also vengeful, unjust, merciless and sadistic.

The Buddha advised us not to concern ourselves with such speculations, as these speculations are ultimately unproductive. He tells the story of a person who pierced by a poisoned arrow, did not want the arrow to be removed until he knew who shot the arrow, why he was shot, and what kind of poison was on the arrow.

Just as it is a doctor's job to remove the poisoned arrow and treat the wound, and not answer the man's untimely questions; it is the Buddha's role to show us how to free ourselves from suffering and not answer such speculative questions. Thus, He said we should think and focus more on what really matters, which is our practice of Buddhism.

So Buddhism doesn't threaten unbelievers with eternal punishment in hell?

Certainly not! Such threats may have been necessary in ancient times to keep people in line, and were used in conjunction with the promise of rewards in heaven. This kind of approach was also used to get people to join particular religious groups, with threats of eternal punishments and assurances of rewards.

Buddhists do not accept the concept of a jealous god who punishes his creations just because they choose a different religion. Practically all civilized nations respect and guarantee the freedom of religious thought and practice, as enshrined in the U.N. Charter (Article 18). Torture furthermore, is banned by all civilized nations on earth. So how can any god that supposedly created all of us be any less civilized? Thus, Buddhists find such threats of eternal torture in hell quite hard to believe.

For example, what kind of being will send or allow another being to burn in a fiery hell for ever and ever? Take a simple lighted match for example. Just hold it under your palm. Can you tolerate the pain for just a few seconds? Can you hold that match under someone's palm for just one minute watching them scream in agony? Can you do that to anyone for all of eternity? Such viciousness is beyond imagination.

Furthermore, if it is in your power to stop such intense and endless suffering, would you not do so? Would any sane and rational being not do so? There can never be any justification for such merciless cruelty for any possible reasons and under any conceivable circumstances.

The Buddha never used any threats, or tried to force anyone to accept His Teachings. He believed in freedom of thought. He recognized that not everyone will accept His Teachings, and that people progress differently and will choose different paths for themselves. He preferred to explain His Teachings in a logical and reasonable manner, and wanted people to understand and realize the Teachings for themselves without fear of any punishments from Him.

Buddhism is not about threats or rewards, but about knowledge and understanding.

> **Albert Einstein :**
> "Buddhism has the characteristics of what would be expected in a cosmic religion for the future : it transcends a personal God, avoids dogmas and theology; it covers both the natural and spiritual, and it is based on a religious sense aspiring from the experience of all things, natural and spiritual, as a meaningful unity. If there is any religion that would cope with modern scientific needs, it would be Buddhism."

Meditation and evil spirits

Does meditation allow demons or evil spirits to enter and possess the mind?

Meditation has been practiced in many different forms, and by many different cultures for thousands of years. It is taught and practiced all over the world and is gaining much popularity, especially in Western countries.

Large international corporations are sending their staff and executives for lessons and retreats in increasing numbers. They recognize the benefits of meditation to be improved concentration and clarity of mind, as well as better management of stress, pain, aggravation and anger.

Neuroscientists at the University of Massachusetts Medical School, by studying the brain waves of people who meditate regularly, have shown that they are more peaceful and tranquil than non-meditators. Researchers at the University of California, San Francisco Medical Centre, have shown that because of meditation, Buddhists really are happier and calmer than most other people!

Some people might discourage us from practicing meditation because of their own irrational fears. It would be wise to treat such talk as superstitious nonsense.

Gays and lesbians

Can gays and lesbians become Buddhists?

Sexual orientation is of no great importance in Buddhism. The Buddha would ask, who is better - a morally upright gay or a crooked and dishonest heterosexual? To the Buddha, what counts is the morality and virtue of a person, and whether or not that person is on the Path towards enlightenment.

Therefore, gays and lesbians who lead virtuous lives can most certainly become Buddhists.

Smoking and Buddhism

Is smoking against Buddhism?

Strictly speaking, Buddhism would not consider smoking to be morally incorrect.

However, serious practitioners of Buddhism who are already on this habit usually attempt to give it up. This is because smoking is a severe form of craving and attachment as it is extremely addictive. Also, smoking is harmful to oneself, as well as to others via the effects of second hand smoke. Thus if something is harmful to oneself and also to others, it cannot be viewed positively in Buddhism.

Ambition and contentment

Buddhism teaches contentment, but people have ambitions in work and also want better lives for their families. How can this be reconciled?

While it is true that Buddhism considers contentment to be a virtue, it also realizes that everyone may take different paths to attain their own peace and happiness. In such cases, the Buddha would recommend taking the Middle Path.

Be not too ambitious that you may cause harm or hurt to others in achieving your ambitions. And also don't be too contented that your own livelihood and family be adversely affected.

Vegetarianism, monks and mock meat

Is being vegetarian a must for Buddhists?

In Buddhism, being vegetarian or not depends entirely on the individual. What is emphasized in Buddhism is not the purity of the diet, but the purity of the mind.

Of course, many Buddhists eventually realize the cruelty involved in eating meat, which is nothing more than the flesh of helpless animals. Many succeed in eliminating the craving and attachment to eating meat, and eventually become vegetarian on their own accord.

However, if becoming vegetarian is not convenient or too difficult, then take the path you are comfortable with. Nonetheless, being vegetarian at least once or twice a month is a good way of practicing compassion for all living beings, by consciously abstaining from meat for that day at least.

A book which deals extremely well with the Buddhist perspective on vegetarianism is Philip Kapleau's "To Cherish All Life".

Why do some monks eat meat?

The Buddha refused to prohibit the eating of meat among his followers. He had very practical reasons for this because sufficient vegetable food may not be available in some areas, or could be very scarce in times of drought. For example, vegetable food is extremely limited in places like Tibet.

Monks survive on alms and if alms were restricted to only vegetarian food, then this could be a great burden on the lay people supporting the monks. Thus monks eat whatever they are given, even if it is meat, as long as the animals were not specially killed for them.

Nowadays though, many monks and temples do have a preference for vegetarian food. However, it should be noted that most monks in the Mahayana tradition are strict vegetarians.

Aren't Buddhist vegetarians who eat mock meat hypocritical? Why have mock meat at all?

Mock meat is a popular vegetarian food made from gluten, soybeans or mushrooms which simulate the appearance and taste of real meat. Buddhist vegetarians are sometimes accused of being hypocritical as they profess to avoid meat and yet eat all kinds of such mock meat. Vegetarians generally do not wish to eat anything which involves the suffering and killing of helpless animals. Thus, they do not view mock meat as 'meat', but only as something giving variety to their diet.

Mock meat was originally produced to attract non-vegetarians to vegetarian food. For example, it can be taken by meat eaters wanting to become vegetarian, as such dishes make the transition to being fully vegetarian easier.

In any case, eating mock meat is still infinitely better than eating the actual flesh of animals.

> **The Buddha :**
> "All beings love Life,
>   all beings love Happiness.
>   Taking yourself for comparison,
>   you should neither harm or kill,
>   nor cause to harm or kill another being."

The different realms of existence

What are the different realms of existence, and are they real places?

Traditionally, Buddhists recognize six different realms or planes of existence. These are the Hell, Animal, Hungry Ghost, Demon, Human and Heaven realms. Some of these realms, such as the Animal and Hungry Ghost realms, overlap our realm.

It is said that there are also different 'levels' within the Heaven and Hell realms. To put this in perspective, take our own world as an example. There are currently 193 countries in the world, spread over seven continents. Living in a peaceful country with a pleasant climate is a far cry from being in a war-torn country wracked by hunger and disease. It is clear that even in our own world, there are vast differences between different countries!

Thus a Heaven realm is a plane of existence which is far more agreeable than even the best country in our world, and a Hell realm is a plane where conditions are far harsher than anywhere on earth. Even the different 'levels' within these realms can be compared to different countries in each continent where the living conditions in some countries may be 'better' or 'worse' than others.

There is an alternative viewpoint that the Buddha was speaking allegorically when He was talking of these different realms of existence. For example, a person who is suffering from severe physical disabilities, very serious illnesses, or is mentally deranged may be said to be reborn in a Hell realm. People who undergo lives of deprivation where their only focus is looking for their next meal and staying alive, may be said to be born in the Animal realm.

People who have constant unfulfilled and burning desires and are never satisfied no matter how much they have, may be said to be in the realm of Hungry Ghosts. Those who are overly aggressive and constantly fighting and struggling for power and possessions may be in the Demon realm. And people who are born with great physical beauty and wealth may be said to be reborn in a Heaven realm. For example, sports and movie stars who have all of these attributes along with literally millions of fans or 'worshippers', are often described as gods!

Quite obviously the Lower realms of Hell, Animals, Hungry Ghosts and Demons are places of suffering, and the Heavenly realms are places of enjoyment. However, the Buddha says that these realms are not particularly suitable places for the practice of Buddhism, or to accumulate positive kamma. This is because the beings in the Lower realms are usually in too much suffering, and the Heavenly beings are too busy enjoying themselves.

Therefore, because the Human realm has both suffering and happiness, it can be considered the most suitable place to learn and practice the Buddha's Teachings. Also, it is the Human realm that offers the greatest opportunity to do good and accumulate positive kamma.

However, the Buddha also said that many Heavenly beings do practice His Teachings and are able to achieve Nibbana. He therefore encouraged everyone to strive for a good rebirth in either a Heavenly or Human realm.

Whether these six realms of existence are actual or figurative doesn't really matter. What really matters is to maintain the practice so as to ensure a good rebirth. This is very important as it is only in either a Human realm or a Heavenly realm that we are able to learn and practice the Buddha's Teachings, and thus attain Nibbana.

Western celebrity Buddhists

With Buddhism becoming more popular in the West, are there any well-known personalities who have become Buddhists?

There are in fact many high-profile personalities who have discovered and taken up Buddhism. The following are just a few of the more well-known celebrity Buddhists :

Richard Gere	Movie Star
Harrison Ford	Movie Star
Orlando Bloom	Movie Star
Keanu Reeves	Movie Star
Uma Thurman	Movie Star
Oliver Stone	Film Producer
Tina Turner	Pop Singer
Adam Yauch	Pop Singer
Herbie Hancock	Jazz Musician
Tiger Woods	Champion Golfer
Roberto Baggio	Soccer Star
Phil Jackson	NBA Coach
William Ford Jr.	Chairman, Ford Motor Co.

DAILY PRACTICE

Salutation, Taking Refuge, and the Five Precepts

There are no hard and fast rules but a good daily practice would be to start with paying respects to the Buddha, the Taking of Refuge, then taking the Five Precepts. You can do this before a Buddha image, but it doesn't really matter if you don't have one.

You can pay respects to the Buddha and express gratitude for His Teachings by reciting with sincerity, the traditional salutation three times :

> Honour To Him, The Blessed One,
> The Worthy One, The Fully Enlightened One.

Or in Pali :

> Namo tassa, bhagavato, arahato, samma-sambudhassa.

Traditionally, Buddhists affirm themselves to be such by reciting the Taking of Refuge in the 'Triple Gem' of the Buddha, the Dhamma and the Sangha. As you recite this, it may help to mentally visualize the Buddha, teaching the Dhamma, to the Sangha :

> To the Buddha I go for Refuge;
> To the Dhamma I go for Refuge;
> To the Sangha I go for Refuge.

For the second time, to the Buddha I go for Refuge;
For the second time, to the Dhamma I go for Refuge;
For the second time, to the Sangha I go for Refuge.

For the third time, to the Buddha I go for Refuge;
For the third time, to the Dhamma I go for Refuge;
For the third time, to the Sangha I go for Refuge.

Taking the Five Precepts would be simply reciting and mentally resolving to try your best to keep these basic rules of morality:

1. I undertake the Precept to abstain from killing any living beings.
2. I undertake the Precept to abstain from taking what is not given.
3. I undertake the Precept to abstain from sexual misconduct.
4. I undertake the Precept to abstain from lying and false speech.
5. I undertake the Precept to abstain from the abusive consumption of intoxicants and drugs.

Meditation

If there is time for meditation, then some people go straight into practicing the form of meditation they choose such as Vipassana meditation, while others may start by doing some Metta meditation first. Alternatively, many prefer to do Metta meditation after the main session as the mind is then more calm and focused. Again, these are all individual choices, and keep in mind that even a short meditation session can be very beneficial.

It will be good however, to occasionally devote some meditation sessions specially to Metta meditation. This is to cultivate the qualities of Loving-Kindness and Compassion, and to radiate Metta not only to people who are close to you, but also to all sentient beings in existence whether they are small, medium or large, visible or invisible, near or far, etc.

Sharing of Merits

Meditation is a wholesome action, and reaps positive kamma. An excellent way to conclude a meditation session would be to share this positive kamma with others, also known as the practice of sharing merits.

Just mentally share the good kamma you have accumulated with all beings, and also with any departed relatives you may have. This enables one to cultivate generosity, and also allows all sentient beings to share in the happiness of your positive actions.

In fact, sharing merits can be done after any kind of good deeds. For example, after you have done some voluntary services to help the less fortunate, after making a donation to help the old, poor or sick, or even after talking about the Dhamma with anyone interested.

Everyone goes through ups and downs in life. In times of stress and difficulty, more emphasis can be placed on practicing Metta meditation and the sharing of merits. If need be, after these practices, you can mentally request the help of any beings that may be able to assist you in the trying times you could be facing.

Depending also on your past kamma, it may be possible that things will soon start to change for the better. If so, don't forget to be grateful and give thanks!

Mindfulness

Something often overlooked but extremely valuable is the constant practice of mindfulness, or 'sati'. This is related to the practice of Vipassana or Insight meditation which gradually increases self-awareness and the ability to see things as they really are. This practice has been shown to have significant health benefits by enabling one to better manage and control stressful situations.

Sati can be practiced not only during meditation, but as much as you can throughout the day or night. Just be aware whenever you can remember to do so, of your bodily postures and movements whether you are standing, walking, sitting or even lying down. Even to merely be aware, at any one point in time, that you are breathing is a large step forward.

Be aware of your physical sensations (through the five senses), your thoughts, feelings and emotions. Observe all these phenomena, and note in a non-judgmental manner, whether they are positive, negative or even neutral.

It is simply a 'stepping-back' or observing with awareness whatever is happening. For example, when the phone rings, be aware of your hearing the sound, your intention to answer it, the physical movement of reaching for the phone, etc. You can even try to make yourself fully aware that you are walking from one room to another room in your house!

A further example is when you feel anger rising. Simply take a step back and observe. Take your attention away from the person or situation you are angry with and just acknowledge the anger as 'anger'. Look for the source of the anger within yourself, why and at what you are angry with, and even try to 'measure' the intensity of your anger.

It will not be easy but eventually you will be able to observe how anger arises and how it fades away. In time you will quite easily be able to remain calm and mindful in the face of just about any frustrations and difficulties.

The emphasis is on self-awareness in the 'present moment'. The past, even of a minute ago, is dead and gone. The future is yet to occur, and may not be at all as expected. The idea is not to dwell in the past, or dream of the future. Observe and live each present moment as it comes about. You will then be truly living and able to see life as it really is.

Learn and share the Dhamma

If you have the time, try to learn at least some Dhamma each day. And as in all good things, share it also with anyone interested.

The Buddha said that the only way to repay our parents for bringing us into this world and taking care of us from birth, is to teach and instil them in the Dhamma.

For those who have children, one of the greatest things you can possibly do for them is to share your knowledge in the Dhamma, and give them a good foundation in the Teachings.

When you share the Dhamma, it is a gift for this life as well as for many, many lives to come.

Be Kind

Finally, always be open, patient and humble. Treat everyone with respect, and everything with kindness.

The Dalai Lama :
"My religion is simple. My religion is kindness."

With the practice of Dana, Sila and Bhavana, the Buddha has given us the guidelines on how to obtain peace and happiness in this life, a favourable rebirth for the next life, and in time the joy and freedom of Nibbana.

These guidelines are quite easy to follow and are not too difficult for everyday practice.

Everyone makes mistakes so if you fall back once in a while, don't worry too much about it, just keep trying.

Try out the path of the Buddha for yourself!

LETTERS FROM AROUND THE WORLD

This booklet is dedicated to all those who had written these wonderfully inspiring and heartwarming letters. Apologies to the many people whose letters I have not had space to be included here.
My gratitude and thanks are extended to all.

This site is so special because I have been to hundreds of Buddhist sites and I found myself being drawn back to this one again and again. Perhaps its the way it is laid out. Its put together in such a way that anyone can understand it. The Buddha taught differently in different areas so persons of all walks of life could understand him. Again many thanks! May peace be with you always brother!
Sincerely yours, **Kenny**
Indiana, USA

I have just found your site, it is amazing. After a rather awful introduction to Buddhism, I almost fell off the path. Your site is so very easy to understand and to navigate, this will now be a much visited site. Thank you so much for writing so that the English speaking among us can finally understand the very basic, simple way of Buddhism.
With Metta, **Maeve**
Queensland Australia

First I want to say thank you. Words cannot express the kindness that you have shown me and the rest of the world. You have given so many wonderful words and gifts of wisdom, to all who ask of you. I only hope that my journey will be as blessed and filled with knowledge. I sent my sister to your website, and that was the start of her journey in a new direction. Thank you...

Tiana Hill
California, USA

Thank you very much for the wonderful and meaningful gift that you had given to me last week. On behalf of my family I would like to say Sadhu Sadhu Sadhu to you. Your generous approach and the humour that you have created will enhance the Buddhist youth and the future generation to be more interested with the Buddhist way of life. Keep it up with your good effort in promoting the humble approach towards the Buddha Dhamma as a way of life. Thank you.

Mr. Yen Kim Pok
Melaka, West Malaysia

Your website is very recommendable! Great explanations: short, to the point, not evasive but clear. Very often I find your explanations easy to grasp for 'newcomers' to Lord Buddha's teachings - simply put: SADHU!

Mr Lennart Lopin
Hamburg, Germany

I wish to thank you most sincerely for sending me the package of booklets and stickers. I received them at school and my teaching colleagues were so very interested in the items enclosed. A deep and meaningful and very open discussion followed as to the beauty of Buddhism. Again, thank you very much and my blessings to you. Kindest regards,

Lee Griffith
Bribie Island, Australia

Greetings and sincere thanks! I received the box from you yesterday and just finished opening it. I was so excited. Thank you very much for sending all of this. I am deeply grateful. My daughter lives in Wisconsin, USA, and I'll be sending her a copy of what you sent me. I think she will find that the information and teachings will really help her.

I cannot say "Thank You" enough. I have several friends with whom I want to share these precious gifts you have sent. Cause and effect are interesting and all about life and death and all that's impermanent, I suppose. I'm just grateful for you and for the "cause" of your compassion. May your blessings be as numerous as the stars in the heavens.

Sincerely, Barbara
Texas, USA

Hi, I have received my package today, thank you. I have thought of Buddhism for a number of years and only recently have realised that this is the spiritual path I want to travel, and certainly I am still struggling. I find your site very easy to understand, things that I need explaining seem to get clarified. The books are easy to read, and at night before I sleep seems to be the best time to read. I have not yet gone to a Temple, I would like to. It would be great to keep in touch.

Respectfully yours,
Elaine
Belfast, N. Ireland

Hello and thanks for the free materials you have sent me. To send those items at no cost shows much care and compassion and this makes me embrace Buddhism even more. Thank you and may peace and happiness be full in your lives.

Dustin
Michigan, USA

Wow...what a wonderful website... truly a breath of fresh air.
Adam B.
Los Angeles, CA

Your books, stickers, CDs are nice and useful and I really enjoy them. I am going to find out more about Buddhism myself and to share the stuff with my friends as there is little information on Buddhism here in Lithuania.
Thank you very much!   Best wishes,
Lukas
Lithuania

I received the package you sent two days ago. Thank you! I live in a rural area with little access to any religion but Christianity. I'm very excited about learning more about Buddhism. Thanks so much,
Hillary
Wisconsin, USA

Thank you so much for the CDs, etc. The Metta CD has given me so much peace, I'm sleeping better and no nightmares. I go to Rigpa Meditation Centre in Limerick every Wednesday, and I have brought the CDs and books in with me to help spread the Dharma. Newcomers to Rigpa find them easy to understand. I can deal with stress, I'm happier, my brother's death 2 years ago brought me even closer to Buddhism. Thank you again. I have told everyone in the Centre about your website and I often see people writing down the web address from my bumper sticker. May you be happy, may you be well.
Sharon Roche
Ireland

Beautifully done! Has helped me considerably to understand Buddhist concepts more clearly. Thank you so much for putting together and maintaining this site, it's wonderful!
Regards, Andy
Lewes, UK

Thank you so much. I've stumbled across your site unintentionally but I'm so happy I did. I need more directed practice in my life and have been seeking this for a very long time.
Elizabeth Zimmers
Cupertino, USA

I am just approaching Buddhism, and, even in Italy we have good teachers and courses about it. I have found your website so clear, interesting and even humorous that I feel at ease with your words and way of explaining. Thanks again and Best wishes.
Lorena Susanna
Italy

I must say again how much I enjoy your website. There are bigger and more in depth websites, but yours just has a very nice feel about it. It feels good. Everything is straight to the point and nothing is complicated or condescending. "Sweet and Simple", as we sometimes say in the USA. Please keep up the good work on the website!
Pete Johnston
USA

Congratulations on a super site.......
No reason at all why we cannot have a 21st. century attitude to a 2500 year old philosophy. Love and Light to you and all your team.
David Wiliams
Lübeck, Germany

Thank you for the booklets and CDs you've sent. We've been meditating for some time, after going through your booklets and CDs we've switched to metta meditation and since then we have been healing and tuning ourselves to be better human beings. We think that you have shown us a true way. Sincerely, we came to your site not by mere chance. You are doing a great job and we are extending our deep gratitude and best wishes to you.

Jiotee and Karan
Mauritius

Thank you, Thank you, Thank you for the wonderful site. I have been interested in Buddhism for some time as an alternative to more "negative" religions. As I learn more about Buddhism through your site I have the strongest desire to WEEP. I have found my true beliefs echoed in a religion embraced by so many!

Sara Mathews
Pensacola, Florida

Your site is great. It is not only helping me understand more about Buddhist teachings but is also helping me get my head round what I actually believe. Whenever someone asked me before about what I believe I wouldn't know what to say. This site has helped me come to decisions about what I believe and how I should live my life. Thank you so much.

Isobel McMillan
England

I've always felt Buddhism is what I've been looking for. It's my missing link. I've also only just found your site and read through it. I really enjoyed it so much.

Rosemary Blackwood
N. Ireland

Just wanted you to know that I received all the great stuff you sent. Thank you so very much. I love going through your web site and have sent it on to others. I've been interested in learning more about Buddhism for a while and your web site is so "user-friendly", it makes visiting your site a pleasure. Thank you again.
Judy Roberts
Arizona, USA

I have read a great deal of your website, and I wanted to tell you: it is the most comprehensive primer on Buddhism I have found. (And I work in a college library.)
I am very interested in Buddhism, and you have helped me tremendously. Thanks again!
LeAnn Glenn
Texas, USA

Thank you very much for creating a beautiful place for us to update our knowledge on Buddhism & also to collect merits by helping you to distribute the truth (Dhamma) among human. Merits will help us for our present & future lives in the universe. May the Triple Gem Bless You !
Rohan Piyatilake
Sri Lanka

I am sharing the message of Buddha with my children and soon their friends. Your free materials along with the literature I have already purchased will be of great help.
Thank You and Namaste.
David Blanche
U.S.A.

What an amazing website! I feel very brave and safe after reading this. I hope everyone on the earth would have read this too.
Myitzu
Singapore

I just want you to know that your site has some of the best info I have come across regarding Buddhism. It is presented in nice little bites, so it's not as overwhelming as most of the info I have read before. It's simple, engaging, and very helpful. I learned a lot from your site, and for that, I am grateful. Thank you!
Becki Pyatt
Salem, USA

Thanks for the wonderful books and CDs you have sent to me. As Chairman of the Multi-Faith Alliance and Co-Organiser for the London Buddhist meet-up Group I fully support and appreciate the wonderful work you are doing. And I send prayers and good wishes to you and for the continuation of your excellent Work. May You and all beings find True Happiness, Good Health and Great Wisdom.
Richard Askew
London, England

Thank you for your wonderful site - I and my son have been looking for information on Buddhism - to help and guide us on our chosen path - which your site has done. Thank you so much.
Penelope Clark
England

Wonderful site! Well made, informative - thank you! We in the West where the Dhamma has arrived can learn very much from the kindness and generosity of our friends in the East.
With Metta,
Mark
Belgium

I have recently taken a very keen interest in Buddhism and have been researching and reading all about it. A lot of people have been asking me about my findings and my new beliefs and it's been quite exciting. Thank you for having such a well informed website and thank you for offering these items up to help spread the word of Buddhism.

Paul Garrett
Dallas, USA

I am taking to calling myself a Buddhist, maybe a "bad" Buddhist would be a better description, as I have a lot to learn. But that commitment has now been made OPENLY as a result of your website and the material you offer. Thank you SO much, particularly for making things more understandable than ever before. It really makes a difference to my life, relationships and state of mind.

Kim (Smith)
Philippines

Thank you for your many kindnesses. I attended temple for the first time in my life.
Something wonderful is happening to me. My wife encouraged me through a friend of hers who is a nun. It all makes sense now. SO many things. I can't quite get my Western mind around all of it somehow but already in just two weeks I have a deep peace and a loving compassion for all things living. I am blessed because of the Buddha, the Dharma, and the Sangha (like you) !
Bless you forever, may you find great joy! Thank you!

Tim L. Kellebrew
Portland, USA

Thank you so much for the booklets and CDs and DVDs. I received them on Friday and I have been hooked on them ever since. Long time ago I either read or heard that when you are ready, the teacher will come. So thank you again. With best regards,
Helena
Finland

Been searching since 1980 when I was conscripted into the army. My search for the right religion or way of life has been long and intense. This is the most helpful and inspirational site I have ever come across. I have studied many religions but have been slowly gravitating towards Buddhism. I have printed the first stage of meditation training and will begin tonight. Suddenly this makes sense to me. Weird, as I have many books on Buddhism. This may sound cheezy but from this moment on I will start to study and practise in earnest. Maybe someday I will be able to tell you how many temples churches mosques etc I have been to. Thank you, thank you, thank you.
Doug Bishop
South Africa

I just wanted to say THANK YOU! for providing this free website with informative and helpful information about Buddhism. As a new believer, I found it very fulfilling! Thank You!
Randee Hartman
United States of America

A GREAT site, I am just learning about Buddhism and the help that this site has personally given me is brilliant. It is comforting to know that there are people out there who will help you if you need it.
Sam Broom
United Kingdom

This is just the kind of information I was searching for today. Thank you for you giving heart...
Mr.Steven C. Englert
United States of America

Again I have to say your site is great. I've followed Buddhism for many years now but every so often there's a grey spot or two. Your site clarifies these grey spots and suddenly everything makes sense. Thank you,
Noel
Queensland, Australia

Thank you for making such an understandable and "down to earth" site on such a spiritual subject. It will be of great use especially to those not very familiar with Buddhism and wanting to orientate themselves on it.
Ginou
Albuquerque, United States

I am just so glad I found T Y and the beautiful "free stuff" I can give away to people. Being quite new to Buddhism, it is lovely to share the Dhamma with friends and family so that they can understand better. With Metta,
Freya Marshall
Kent, England

I have received the parcel you sent, and I am very happy with the contents. The website you keep is not only informative, but very inspiring for one who is so far away from a temple. Sir, I thank you so much for your work in spreading the teachings of the Buddha. Bless you this day. At your service,
Christopher Reyes
Texas, USA

This is a most interesting website. I am a student in the Philosophy of Religion and am drawn to Buddhism. I think you are doing potential students a great favour here. I support this website and everything it stands for. May your website and your life's work flourish over many lifetimes. Grace and peace be upon you.

Raymond
Hong Kong

Please send me some of your decals so that I may spread the word. Your website is so amazing and beautiful, more people need to know about this! Namaste,

Emily
USA

I came across your website by accident, but was drawn by the title! I have been looking for years to find the impossible "truth" but never got close. I have always thought of Buddhism as being the one for me. Now I will definitely read further. It's as if I have arrived home!! Thank you. May peace and happiness guide your footsteps.

Mike Maynard
Spain

Buddhism has been so good to me, that I find it hard not to share with my loved ones. I will make sure to pass along your website to everyone and anyone that may have questions. It is a blessing to have websites like yours that can enlighten others to a wonderful new beginning. Thank you so much for all that you have done. Happiness Always,

Shana
Virginia, USA

BASIC MEDITATION PRACTICE

Preface by Piya Tan

Meditation is the best immunization you can have, that is, for health more than just for the body. It helps you to centre your mind and in that way to clear it so that you see yourself in the right perspective, and get your life's priorities right. Meditation reminds you that happiness, like the truth, is not out there, but right in here, in your mind and heart.

You have a choice: let something or someone outside you control your mind and your life, or be in charge of yourself and rightly, too. This is what meditation does.

Brother T Y Lee has provided spiritual water for the thirsty; he has even brought these quenching waters to you with his free books, and other Buddhist materials, all for free — simply because they are priceless. As the saying goes: you can bring a horse to water, but it must want to drink.

If you wish to take that one inner step, seek an experienced and upright teacher (make sure you check him or her out first), and learn how to mind the mind. Meditation is like learning to drive: you cannot effectively drive with just a driving manual (even the best). A living practitioner is the best guide, and in no time you will be able to drive your own life, and even show the way to others.

The "Just Be Good" website has a simple philosophy and approach: Buddhism is very simple to start with if you desire happiness. If you really want to be happy, start with being good to yourself. That means, taking care of not only your body but also your mind: a healthy mind in a healthy body.

Yet you cannot be truly happy if others around you are not happy. Spread that goodness, and your own happiness will grow many times over.

Goodness and happiness are like love: you only have it when you give it away.

May we, like Brother Lee, be able to give more: but it starts here.

Piya Tan
[The Minding Centre & Pali House, Singapore]
25th December 2006

BASIC MEDITATION PRACTICE

A Practical Guide for Beginners and Instructors

By Piya Tan
©1983, 3rd rev ed ©2006

1. WHAT IS MEDITATION?

In Buddhism, "meditation" is best rendered as mental cultivation or mind training (remembering that the body is also involved). Through meditation, your mind, indeed your whole life, goes through spiritual growth – your mind becomes clear so that better self-understanding can arise. You become more wholesomely aware of yourself, of others, of your environment and ultimately of true reality itself.

Meditation makes you happy simply for yourself. There is this beautiful and powerful stillness in the centre of your life despite the storm around you.

Meditation as taught by the Buddha has two aspects: calmness or concentration, that is, the unification of the mind, and insight wisdom. I teach the **mindfulness of breathing** and **the cultivation of loving-kindness**, as the anchor practices. "Anchor" in the sense that they give you stability and grounding, so that you have a good way of knowing your progress.

Most people need to begin with cultivating calmness – the "stop" aspect of meditation, or learning to let go of mental hindrances or distractions as they arise. These distractions usually come in the form of obsessive and reactive negative mental habits (lust, ill-will, worry, drowsiness, and doubt).

As the mind becomes more and more calm, and your mind become more and more focused, you will, in due course, get flashes of insight into the true nature of things – insight wisdom has arisen. This is the "realize" aspect of meditation. You then begin to see the three characteristics of all existence: impermanence, unsatisfactoriness and insubstantiality.

2. GETTING STARTED

The best way to get started in meditation is to attend a meditation class led by an experienced teacher. When you feel ready, you might like to go for a meditation retreat. A good retreat is one where there are ideal, or at least conducive, physical and mental conditions for personal development.

However, the following may act as a guide for those who would like to get started but who may not have access to a teacher or who are far from a temple or meditation centre.

a) A disciplined life

Before even getting started in meditation, it is recommended that one begin by leading a morally upright and disciplined life.

Basically, a disciplined life is based on the keeping of the Five Precepts, the minimal lay Buddhist code of conduct, that is, the avoidance from harming life, from stealing, from unhealthy and illicit sexual conduct, from lying, and from drinking and addictive habits. For non-Buddhists, these are basic life guides: respect life, let live, respect others, respect truths that help, and above all respect your mind.

Your preparation for meditation also includes the ridding of guilt and doubt from your mind, and leading a regulated life. If you have any guilty feelings over some action or thought, it is good to get them straightened out as best you can. Any doubt regarding doctrine or practice should be cleared up or at least not thought about at this early stage.

b) Proper clothing and food

Simple and loose clothing that covers most of your body are best. It would be wise to have some warm clothing on the ready too, if you are in a cool place. Try to have your own meditation cushion or stool (proper sitting postures will be discussed under topic 4). Otherwise, you could fold or roll up your blanket to serve as a cushion.

Proper eating habit are very helpful. Too much food causes heaviness and drowsiness, while too little might weaken you. Unhealthy food may have a disturbing effect on you, and it is worth remembering that chewing food well helps digestion (and is also a practice of mindfulness).

c) Conducive environment

The place of meditation should be isolated, peaceful and safe. A beautiful natural surrounding helps greatly. Good places for meditation retreats may be a shelter in a quiet mountain, a remote, or a peaceful temple. Otherwise, a quiet space in your house can also be used for meditation. The best time to meditate is when you feel like doing it.

Make sure you get enough rest but not too much sleep. Healthy exercise takes the form of a daily walk or yoga, or simple stretching. If you are at a retreat, try not to read at all as this tends to cloud and excite your mind and thus hinder your ability to meditate properly.

d) Personal freedom

If you have had a hectic time, it is good to first let go of all thoughts of unfinished business, relatives, friends, social activities and studies pulling you away from your meditation. Make a complete break with the world! Very important: always switch off your phones, even the silent mode, so that nothing will disturb your inner peace.

e) Spiritual friends

Your communication with others should be as positive as possible. This will ensure a generally peaceful state of mind and also help provide emotional support for our practice. Your practice will be greatly enhanced if you feel in good contact with those you regard as your spiritual friends.

3. PRELIMINARY PREPARATIONS

A beginner would usually find it difficult jumping straight into a meditation session. If you like, you could start with a few basic chantings you are familiar with before meditating. Or you could have a short period of "just sitting" before the session proper. Otherwise, you could start off by having a relevant reading from your meditation guide-book (such as "Piya's Meditation Guide").

In a humid climate, you should pay extra attention to personal hygiene and cleanliness. A wash before meditation would not only be refreshing but also keep away mosquitoes (which are attracted by sweat and body odour).

If you are in a new place, it is good to always begin with loving-kindness, spreading a wholesome aura all around.

4. SITTING POSTURE

(a) LEGS – The best position is in **the full-lotus posture**, that is, if you are used to this or know yoga. Sit on a flat cushion and cross your legs, with the dorsum of each foot lying on the opposite thigh. If this is difficult, then try the **half-lotus posture**. The left foot is on the floor and the right on the left thigh. (It is advisable here to alternate the positions of the feet and thigh after a long session.)

If this method, too, is difficult, then try the the "quarter-lotus" or Bumese posture, that is, both feet on the floor. (One leg should be crossed in front of the other.) It should be noted that these "lotus" positions are easier for people from the East who are used to sitting in these positions from a young age.

Should all these postures prove still difficult, try using one or more meditation cushions, and sit with your knees and lower legs on the floor (with your seat raised higher till you feel comfortable).

As a last resort, try a simple stool or chair (but not a soft cushion that sinks in) and sit very mindfully.

(b) HANDS – Rest them lightly in front of your body, the left hand lying palm upward on the lap and the right hand resting palm upward on the left. Keep the fingers together; the tips of the thumbs lightly touching above the palm.

ARMS – Keep them relaxed and slightly rounded, and held a little away from the body. (If the arms are too close to the body, the resulting warmth will cause drowsiness.)

(c) BACK – Keep it straight, especially the lumbar region. This not only prevents back-ache, but also helps keep the mind clearer and more alert.

(d) EYES – Keep them closed to avoid distraction. If, however, you are sleepy or drowsy, then keep the eyes half-open, and gaze down the line of the nose towards the tip or right in front (about 45 degrees down, looking on the floor).

(e) MOUTH – Keep the jaw relaxed, the teeth slightly apart or just touching, and the lips gently together.

(f) TONGUE – The tip of the tongue should gently touch the back of the upper teeth and the palate. (This helps control the flow of saliva so that there is no need to swallow frequently. But if you feel a tickle in your throat, keep swallowing and use it as a mindfulness practice.)

(g) NECK – Keep it slightly bent forward. Do not bend it too much or sinking and drowsiness will arise. If too straight, agitation and distraction will result.

THE TWO PRACTICES

5. THE TWO KINDS OF MEDITATION METHODS

Personality problems are more common in our society today than ever before. Two predominant manifestations of such problems are, namely:

(1) Tension and its related problems (eg, anxiety, worry, etc.)
(2) Communication difficulties (eg, anger, aggression, etc.)

For each of these areas of problems, Buddhist meditation has a number of healing methods. Two highly recommended methods (for their practical ease and effectiveness) are, namely:

(1) Mindfulness of Breathing (for the first problem area), and

(2) Cultivation of Loving-kindness (for the second
    problem area).

I. THE MINDFULNESS OF BREATHING

The Mindfulness of Breathing is very effective for counteracting wandering thoughts and bringing calmness to yourself. This method is recommended before any of the other basic methods of meditation because you would find great difficulty trying to meditate if you have not yet learnt to concentrate.

Concentration means the integration (or unifying) of our thoughts (indeed, of yourself) – only too often we find our thoughts are at cross-purposes within yourself! When you focus on your breath, you become aware of yourself breathing in and out in a quite natural manner. In this way, you unify your attention and eliminate wandering thoughts. Furthermore, you feel calm, relaxed, even energized, after the practice.

6. THE PRACTICE PROPER

Stage 1 – COUNT AT THE END OF EACH OUT-BREATH
    Breathe in, breathe out – count "One";
    Breathe in, breathe out – count "Two"; and so on up to "Ten," over and over again, for about five minutes or so.
Stage 2 – COUNT AT THE BEGINNING OF EACH IN-BREATH
    Count "One" - breathe in, breathe out;
    Count "Two" - breathe in, breathe out and so on up to "Ten," over and over again, for about five minutes or so.

Stage 3 – WATCH THE WHOLE BREATHE (FLOW OF BREATH)
    Drop the counting and concentrate only on the breathing.

Stage 4 – WATCH THE POINT OF BREATH
    Concentrate on the ticklish sensation within the nostrils, or

on the upper lip, or at the tip of the nose as the air enters and leaves the nose.

7. ANALYSIS OF THE PRACTICE

Even though there are, in practice, four stages of the breath meditation, there are in theory only three stages, namely: (1) Counting; (2) Connecting; (3) Fixing or contact.

(1) THE COUNTING at the earlier stage helps you to concentrate on the meditation object. Stage 1 is fairly easy to do, but in Stage 2, you have to pay more attention to the breath, especially the moment before the in-breath. These two stages are sometimes called the "quick" method.

If you find difficulty with this "quick" method, there is the "slow" (or double count) method, that is:
Breathe in – count "One," Breathe out – count "One".
Breathe in – count "Two," Breathe out – count "Two," and so on up to "Ten," over and over again, till you are quite calm.

You may count up to any number between 5 and 10: below five is too short for focus; more than 10 can be distracting.
(**Note**: The breath should really be noted as a continuous flow. The counting is just an aid for concentration. If you find the counting simply distracting, do not use it: simply go on to the second stage.)

(2) THE CONNECTION refers to Stage 3, that is, the uninterrupted attention to the in-breaths and out-breaths. You simply allow yourself to become absorbed in the flow of the breath as it comes in and goes out (as it appears to rise and fall, to expand and contract).

(3) THE FIXING OR CONTACT refers to Stage 4, that is, the

physical action of the breath striking or touching the nose-tip or nostril as it enters and leaves the body; or it may be regarded as that physical point where the air strikes, namely, the nose-tip.

At any time, if you feel calm and joyful, you need not use the words any more. Simply experience the calmness and joy directly. Go back to the words only when there is a distraction.

8. OVERCOMING DISTRACTIONS IN BREATH MEDITATION

1. WANDERING MIND. This is very common among beginners and those who try to sit and meditate rather abruptly without sufficient "warming up" – that is, doing a few basic chantings, or simply "just sitting" in absolute silence before actually starting to meditate.

A good antidote for the wandering mind is by watching the "rising and falling" of the belly area around the navel (more exactly, two-fingers' breadth above the navel).

2. UNWHOLESOME THOUGHTS, such as anger, lustful thoughts, drowsiness, restlessness or doubt – these can be overcome by any of the traditional antidotes:

(a) **Displacement**. Cultivating the opposite or a different object, for example, cultivating loving-kindness to replace hatred.

(b) **Aversion training**. Considering the consequences or disadvantages of allowing that unwholesome state to take us over.

(c) **Open mind**. Maintain a "sky-like" attitude, that is, simply disregarding the negative thought – just as it has arisen, even so just letting it disappear on its own accord.

(d) **Thought analysis**. Identifying the cause or define the problem – "What am I angry about?" and so on, or ask "Why am I feeling like this?" and you might often discover that your mind had made it all up.

(e) **Determination**. By sheer determination, restraining or suppressing any negative thoughts.

3. FEAR – Should fear arise during meditation and you are not able to handle it, simply open the eyes or stop the meditation. (If you are not used to darkness, you could leave the lights on while meditating, or have some lights on your shrine if you are sitting in front of one.)

4. MENTAL IMAGES – You might see visions, colours and even hear sounds or get fragrant smells. Regard these things as mind-made – they are projections of your own mind. If fear or any other unwholesome thoughts arise, apply any of the antidotes given earlier. (No matter how beautiful or enjoyable these images or objects may be, it is not wise to "enjoy" them too long – treat them as mind-made and conditioned by yourself, and as such impermanent, unsatisfactory and insubstantial).

5. BLISS – Even if bliss should arise, you should be careful not to be intoxicated by it (but treat it as for the images mentioned under point 4). Swaying of the body may also occur but you should voluntarily stop this movement.

6. PHYSICAL PAIN such as numbness, aches, itchiness, etc. They are usually mind-made (potentiated), or magnified by the mind. If the sensation is tolerable, watch and observe it as a passing phenomenon. Should it prove intolerable, mindfully relieve the pain or quietly adjust your posture (so as not to disturb others who are meditating together with you.

7. ALIENATION – Sometimes you might, after prolonged

breath meditation, have some aversion towards other people or feel "withdrawn" from the world. You then feel alienated (which is really the result of your own personality trait). In this case, it is time that you switched to the cultivation of loving-kindness (see below).

9. NOTE ON THE BREATH

At any time during meditation, it is important that you should not force your breath. (In fact, even if you try to, after a while, it will return to its natural pace.) Your breath should be regulated, that is, not audible, gasping or coarse, but restful. Audible breathing is noisy and distracting. Gasping breath is obstructed and not free, and ties you up in knots. A coarse breath is a result of forced effort and tires you. On the other hand, a restful breath is one that goes at its own natural rhythmic pace.

As the body and mind become more calm during meditation, the breath may automatically become shorter and even so refined that you might not feel it at all. This is nothing to worry about as after a while the breath will "return". You should keep on focusing your attention at the nose-tip ("point of breath"), or have a general awareness of the whole body from the crown of the head to the tip of the toes, or note the contact-points on your body (such as your thumbs touching each other, etc).

10. THE BENEFITS OF BREATH MEDITATION

1. INCREASED AWARENESS which leads to your having greater powers of observation (and also as a result, better memory) and deeper interest in things – indeed, you become more interesting and inspiring yourself. Your senses become more keen and discerning.

2. You feel generally HAPPIER.

3. You may become MORE INTUITIVE AND CREATIVE because a calm and clear mind is fertile for good ideas.

4. The most important benefit is that of liberation from suffering. You will become emotionally independent: you are simply happy for yourself, and as such you have the energy and wisdom to help others too.

II. CULTIVATION OF LOVING-KINDNESS

The cultivation of loving-kindness is especially good for those who have problems resulting from hatred and ill will, those who have difficulty getting along with others and those who harbour self-pity and even self-hate. This practice turns you into a compassionate and radiant person as a start at least.

11. THE PRACTICE PROPER

Stage 1 – YOURSELF. We develop loving-kindness towards ourselves, and mentally say such positive words like:

MAY I BE WELL!
MAY I BE HAPPY!
MAY I BE FREE FROM HATRED!
MAY I MEET WITH SUCCESS ALWAYS!
MAY NO HARM COME TO ME! … And so on…

(You may repeat one or two of these sentences or add in new ones in any way you like – it is not so much the words as the thought that counts.)

Stage 2 – A NEAR AND DEAR FRIEND OR RELATIVE, someone who is still alive. This could be someone who has been very kind to you. Visualize or recollect this person and develop loving-kindness in the same way you did to yourself earlier on.

Stage 3 – A NEUTRAL PERSON. Choose someone you

neither like nor dislike, especially someone whom you meet often and whose face you know well. Show the same loving-kindness to this person as you did to yourself and the dear friend earlier on.

Stage 4 – SOMEONE WITH A PROBLEM. Think of someone that you know who is having some problems or who is unhappy. If your loving-kindness is strong enough, you may even send it to someone who has been hurt, or someone you dislike, even an enemy. Should you be unable to think of such a person, try someone who has done something you disapprove of.

Stage 5 – UNIVERSALIZING THE LOVING-KINDNESS. First of all, we line up all four kinds of persons mentally before you: self, near and dear friend, neutral person and enemy, and we develop the same loving-kindness equally towards them all.

Then we direct the same loving-kindness towards everyone in the room in which we are meditating (if in a retreat) – and then everyone in the same building; all the people in the locality; all the people in the city; in the country. Then we proceed continent by continent, going all the way round the world, filling the whole world with loving-kindness.

Finally we radiate our loving-kindness to all beings in different parts of the universe – east, west, north, south, above, below and across.

12. ANALYSIS OF THE PRACTICE

The five stages of the cultivation of loving-kindness practice start off with the easiest, getting gradually more difficult and ending up with the most important stage – the "universalizing". In this practice, you should begin with yourself because you are often not pleased with yourself. Consciously or unconsciously, there are times when you indulge in self-defeat, self-pity, and even self-hate (eg, when you feel that you are not doing as well as others). If you cannot love yourself, you will find it very difficult to love other people.

In the second stage, we develop loving-kindness towards a near and dear person who is still living. Be careful when you think of someone close (like a spouse or partner), so that lust does not arise instead: this will weaken your focus. Thinking of a dead person usually invokes sorrow, if not, fear or speculative thinking. (Such persons can be put in the last stage.)

In the third stage, we think of a neutral person whom we have seen often but towards whom we have no particular feeling (whether liking or disliking). Such a person may be of either sex (but should any unwholesome thoughts arise, you should immediately change to some other person.)

The fourth stage – thinking well of an enemy – can be difficult for some people. In that case, you should consider the disadvantages of having an enemy and that hatred is really a negative emotion within yourself (and therefore hurts you more than anyone else). You might start by visualizing the present enemy together with yourself in friendlier days and start off the fourth stage from there wishing the hostile person well and so on.

13. "BREAKING THE BARRIERS"

The most important stage in the loving-kindness practice is the fifth stage. The previous four stages are really preparatory leading to this essential stage. When a meditator succeeds in developing loving-kindness that is equal with regards to himself, a dear person, a neutral person and an enemy, he is said to have **broken down the barriers** between himself and others.

As you go on radiating loving-kindness to a greater number of people over a greater area, you might (if you like), visualize particular groups of people, or even individuals in, say a particular part of the locality, city, country or world. It should be noted here that you need not stick to the same group or individual all the time. You may visualize anyone (except in the first stage) as the need arises.

14. VISUALIZATION AND RADIATION

To "visualize" here means "call to mind" or "bring before the mind's eye" certain objects such as a person, a category of beings (e.g. animals), a certain area or direction. It means imagining the objects towards which you are radiating your thoughts of loving-kindness.

When visualizing your object of meditation, you may, for instance, imagine your dear friend with his face looking happy and radiant. Then to that visualized image, radiate such thoughts as: "May you be well. May you be happy. May you be free from disease and trouble….." and so on.

By "radiation" is meant an expression or projection of certain wholesome thoughts promoting the well-being of the object in mind. Though you are instructed to "say" sentences like "May I be well" mentally, it is not so much "speaking" that is meant here, but rather feeling the loving-kindness.

15. OVERCOMING DIFFICULTIES IN LOVING-KINDNESS

1. WANDERING MIND or difficulty in concentration during the practice of loving-kindness meditation can be corrected by watching the in-breath and out-breath at the nose-tip till your mind is concentrated again (then you should go back to the point where you left off in the loving-kindness meditation).

2. UNWHOLESOME THOUGHTS should be dealt with in the same manner as prescribed under "Overcoming Distractions

in Breath Meditation" (Section 8, point 2). You should avoid a person or subject that arouses lustful thoughts during loving-kindness meditation.

3. INABILITY TO VISUALIZE THE SUBJECT – You should then try simply thinking of the subject (eg, by mentally saying the name).

4. OTHER DISTRACTIONS such as fear, images, bliss and discomfort should be dealt with as prescribed in the respective paragraphs under "Overcoming Distractions in Breath Meditation".

16 THE BENEFITS OF LOVING-KINDNESS MEDITATION

There are eleven advantages you get after you are fully absorbed in the practice of loving-kindness meditation:

1. COMFORTABLE SLEEP – You get to sleep easily without turning over or even snoring.

2. WAKING IN COMFORT – You get up without groaning, yawning or turning over.

3. NO DISTURBING DREAMS – In your dreams, you would only see auspicious things (like worshipping at a shrine or listening to teachings) or archetypal images (such the Buddha, Guanyin, gods or dieties).

4. OTHER PEOPLE FIND YOU LIKEABLE – You make friends easily and find people easy to cope with.

5. YOU ARE DEAR TO NON-HUMANS – Animals and other non-human beings (such as gods or dieities and "spirits") will not harm or cause fear in you.

6. DIVINE PROTECTION – Divine beings will guard you dearly. (Or, you feel a good ambience everywhere.)

7. PROTECTION AGAINST FIRE, POISON AND WEAPONS – Your own mind of loving-kindness will ward off or nullify the danger or effect of such things.

8. EASY MENTAL CONCENTRATION – You are able to overcome drowsiness or hindrances.

9. SERENE COUNTENANCE – You look radiant and attractive.

10. UNCONFUSED MIND AT DEATH – When death comes, you die in peace as if falling asleep.

11. GOOD REBIRTH – If you do not win spiritual liberation in this life, after death you will be reborn in a high heavenly realm. In simple terms, you will feel renewed and reborn even right here.

17. AVOIDING EXTREMES

There seem to be two separate poles in our experience of our energy: one is lively and dynamic, even hysterical; the other pole, calm and balanced, with the negative extreme of gloominess and drowsiness. For example, when for some reason you lose your basic concentration and your attention becomes more and more scattered, like a ship in a storm that drags its anchor, this is called "drifting". In this case we could have been over-exerting ourselves and a reaction has occurred. It is recommended that you should balance up this active element by regularly doing the "just sitting" practice.

While you are meditating, after a while, for no apparent reason, you "run out of steam". This is sometimes called "sinking," that is, we have come to the end of our energy, and our mental and emotional state becomes increasingly blank and dull. To correct this, you should fix your attention on the nose-tip (and watch the breath there). In the case of the "drifting" mind, your attention should be brought down and fixed on the navel (and watch the rising and falling of the belly).

It is perhaps relevant here to mention how you should end your sitting. Just as after a good run you do not immediately lie flat or jump into the shower, but "warm down," so too after meditation you should not abruptly take up the day's work. It would be good to spend a short while (of at least 5-10 minutes) just being by yourself, in the garden perhaps, silently and mindfully "unwinding" yourself.

18. GOOD PROGRESS

How do you know that you are making good progress in your meditation? The best criterion is that it results in your being calm and that you enjoy your practice. As you improve in meditation, the wandering thoughts begin to disappear, and concentration becomes more and more easy. There is an increasing feeling of pleasure and joy as we involve ourselves more emotionally. We are now entering the first absorption. In this peaceful and pleasurable state, the only thought in our mind is concerned with the meditation object itself.

Balanced practice is another important ingredient for good progress in your meditation. Breath meditation helps you to be more "integrated," more concentrated and calm while loving-kindness meditation makes you more radiant and friendly and able to cope with people. Both practices should be balanced up. Otherwise you would be in danger of developing a zombie-like "alienated awareness" – an awareness in which you do not experience yourself. You become a detached observer who sees, but does not feel; who exists, but is not alive. So keep your practice balanced.

Piya's [non-religious]

Meditation Course
Deep rest, de-stressing, wellness, inner peace

The Minding Centre
http://minding.centre.googlepages.com
Tel: 6569 5205
Blk 644 Bukit Batok Central, #01-68 (2nd flr)
[near Bukit Batok MRT/Interchange] Singapore 650644.

• **Centering the mind**	Mental hindrances & overcoming them.
• **What you see is not what you get**	Making your stress work for you.
• **You are what you think**	Don't let the past autopilot you: live now.
• **Overcoming negative desires**	Healthy emotion in a calm and clear mind.
• **Firewalling your mind**	Healing yourself through lovingkindness.
• **Managing anger**	Self-watching against destructive emotions.
• **Not fearing even fear itself**	Managing your fear and worry.
• **Overcoming drowsiness**	Keeping the mind fresh and attentive.
• **Truly living the moment**	Minding the body: walking meditation.

Close your eyes, see more 👁 The mind sees beyond the eye

Please sign up for with **Ratna Lim** at **6569 5205, Hp 8211 0879**

Piya Tan, the course instructor, who was a monk for 20 years, has been teaching meditation and related fields since 1980s. In 1992, he taught meditation at the University of California at Berkeley, USA. He has taught meditation to corporations such as SIA and HP, & runs deep rest courses for the Defence Science Organization. Currently he conducts weekly and regular classes at the NUS (BS), the Brahm Education Centre and at his own Minding Centre. He lives at Pali House, where he researches and translates the early Buddhist texts (Sutta Discovery series). He teaches the Forest-Insight method of meditation, melding the best of the traditions of Mahasi Sayadaw of Myanmar and of Ajahn Chah of Thailand.

Firefly Mission

…… together we light up the world

Our mission is to build a network of dedicated volunteers to bring forth Universal Love. This covers charity, medicine and education with the spirit of sincerity, integrity, trust and honesty. With love, compassion, joy and selfless giving, volunteers can strive to bring about paradise on earth, through helping the needy, giving joy and eliminating suffering.

The recipients of aid are the materially poor regardless of race, religion and ethnicity. We focus on the poor countrysides of our less developed neighbours such as Bangladesh, Myanmar, Sri Lanka, Nepal, India and Thailand.

Please contact us on how you can help or enrol as a volunteer :

Firefly Mission
3 Hume Avenue, #08-05
Singapore 598719

www.fireflymission.org
enquire@fireflymission.org

"One life's journey, faith is the nourishment, good deeds are a shelter, understanding is the light by day and mindfulness is the protection by night" – Samyutta Nikaya

THE BUDDHA DHAMMA
MANDALA SOCIETY

The BDMS is dedicated to making known the teachings of the Buddha and encouraging its members to apply these teachings to their lives. Through the medium of English, we present the Dhamma in modern terms and in ways that emphasize its relevance to the contemporary world.

The Society publishes books, organizes public talks, meditation classes and activities for young people. The Society's spiritual advisor, Bhante S. Dhammika, is an Australian monk well-known for his writings and public talks.

For more information visit us at 567A Balestier Road, Singapore 329884, or log on to our website at www.bdms.org.sg

You can also get your questions on Buddhism answered by logging on to www.goodquestiongoodanswer.net

BUDDHIST FELLOWSHIP

Who We Are *We are a non-sectarian Buddhist organisation whose vision is to promote Buddha's core teachings and practices and to foster fellowship based on high moral values in the English-speaking community. Our mission is to teach and live the Dhamma in this modern society with minimum rituals, and dispel Ignorance with Compassion and Friendship. We also seek to be a voice of the English-speaking Buddhist community. We are a Buddhist organisation that dares to be different, embarking on revolutionary projects and activities that teach the Dhamma and benefit the community in today's world. We are thus a catalyst of positive change in the Buddhist community in Singapore as we strive to propagate the Dhamma in contemporary language and form.*

What Motivates Us *We believe that everyone of us can make a difference in making this world a better one. It is this belief that motivates us to walk the Buddha's Path in the right manner, by living every moment with greater concern for others than for oneself. Buddhism is not dogmatic but experiential. It is through questioning, analysing, testing and contemplation that we develop our wisdom in order to make the right choices in life. We can help others who go through life making the wrong choices, experiencing confusion, pain and frustrations. Let us walk the Buddha's Path together and be influential examples to all in the world, for there is no better way to share the Truths of Life than to live it and show it.*

Our Activities

Sunday Service: *Morning Service at 11am-12pm, potluck lunch at 12.30-2.00pm*

Wednesday Service: *Evening Service at 7.45pm*

Friday Meditation: *Meditation & "Live" Webcast of Dhamma Talk from BSWA*

Saturday "Moonlight" Service: *Evening Service at 6.00pm, potluck dinner with movies, songs and games!*

Buddhist Fellowship 9 Chwee Chian Road 117488
(Off Pasir Panjang Road, across Pasir Panjang Food Centre)
Tel: (65) 6278 0900 Email: bfellow@singnet.com.sg
Website: www.buddhistfellowship.org

THE BUDDHIST LIBRARY

The Buddhist Library is Singapore's premier centre for the research and study of all aspects of Buddhism. It contains thousands of books in English and Chinese, as well as audio and video resources. The complete sets of the Tipitaka, the sacred scriptures of Buddhism, are also available in English, Pali and Chinese. The Library holds regular talks on the Buddha's teachings, hosts visiting speakers and sponsors other educational, social and spiritual programs.

Opening hours

Tues to Sat : 12.00pm to 9.30pm
Sunday : 10.00am to 9.30pm
Closed on Mondays.

Courses

Wed : Diploma in Buddhist Studies.
Tues & Sat : Postgraduate Diploma in Buddhist Studies.
Fri, Sat & Sun : Master of Arts in Buddhist Studies.

Puja

Every Sunday at 10.00am

Dhamma classes for Children

Sunday : 10.30am to 12.00pm

Free & Easy Meditation

Tuesday : 7.30pm onwards

Yoga classes

Saturday : 9.30am to 12.00pm

For more information and details on coming events contact -
Buddhist Library
2 & 4 Lorong 24A Geylang,
Singapore 398526
Tel : 67468435
Fax : 67417689

Burmese Buddhist Temple

(Mahasasanaramsi)

Existing in Singapore since 1878. Established in 1985
14 Tai Gin Road (Off Ah Hood Road) Singapore 327873
Telephone: 62511717 Website: www.bbt.org.sg
Email: burtempl@singnet.com.sg

REGULAR SERVICES AT BURMESE BUDDHIST TEMPLE

Monday	7 : 30 pm- 9 : 00 pm
	Adult Dhamma Class
Tuesday	7 : 30 pm- 9 : 00 pm
	Abhidhamma Class
Wednesday	8 : 00 pm- 9 : 00 pm
	Puja, Meditation & Dhamma Talk
Friday	7 : 00 pm- 8 : 00 pm
	Adult Meditation Class
Saturday	7 : 30 pm- 9 : 00 pm
	Dhammacakka Chanting (Burmese group)
Sunday	Buddhist Library Opening hours
	10 : 00am- 8 : 00 pm

Chanting/ Meditation (Conducted by Resident Monks)

B.B.T. Sunday Dhamma School

(Teachings are based on Theravada Buddhism Thought and Practice)

9 : 30 am - 10: 00 am	Pali Chanting
10 : 30 am - 11: 00 am	Children's Meditation Class
11 : 00 am - 12: 45 pm	Children's Dhamma Classes
10 : 15 am - 11: 00 am	Maths Tuition for Primary 6 students
10 : 00 am - 12 : 00 pm	Dhamma Talk/ Meditation for Adults
6 : 30 pm - 8 : 00 pm	Children Dhamma Classes (In Burmese)

There are no charges for the attendence of Sunday Dhamma classes
and books provided for the class.
(Free Lunch is provided to all the students after morning class)

Temple opens everyday from 6 : 30 am to 9 : 00 pm.
Individual blessings given by Monks on request. All are welcome.

Majjhima Dhamma Centre
7D, Crane Road, Singapore 429356

Brief History

Majjhima Dhamma Centre (MDC) was formed on 5 May 2007 with the primary intention of promoting and encouraging both Buddhists and non-Buddhists to learn and practice meditation. Through meditation, MDC hopes that members will develop true wisdom through Vipassana meditation and see the Four Noble Truths.

MDC currently has two religious advisors and they are Ven. Phramaha Dr. Sutimon and Ven. Phra Ajahn Chakat. Both Venerables are very learned in the Dhamma and are experienced meditation teachers. Besides meditation, MDC also aims to bring in more English speaking Venerables to Singapore to teach the Buddha's Dhamma-Vinaya.

MDC aims to reach out to both young and old and to bring the teachings of the Buddha to all.

The objectives of MDC are:

a) To promote the teachings (Dhamma) of the Buddha
b) To promote the practice of meditation for the well-being of members
c) To promote charitable and humanitarian activities

Our Activities

- Sutta Classes
- English Dhamma Discussion and Sharing Sessions
- Short courses, seminars and talks on Buddhism
- Buddhist library
- Nightly meditation
- Monthly Weekend Meditation (conducted in conjunction with Uttamayanmuni Buddhist Temple)
- Thai language courses

Contact us:

Email: majjihmadc@gmail.com
Website: www.majjhima.org

Mangala Vihara (Buddhist Temple)

30 Jalan Eunos Republic of Singapore 419495
Telephone: (65) 6744 4285 Fax: (65) 6744 1912
http://www.mangalavihara.org.sg/

Regular Activities at Mangala Vihara (Buddhist Temple):

Daily morning and evening Puja Services
Buddha Puja, Refuge and Precept taking.

Sunday Dhamma Classes for Adults and Children
Students are given a comprehensive understanding of the Dhamma and Abhidhamma in the Theravada tradition through a structured and organised syllabus prescribed by the Colombo YMBA. There are no charges for the attendance of Sunday Dhamma classes and books provided for the classes. Free vegetarian lunch is provided to all the students after class.

For enquiries, please contact:
Ms Clara Lee   : 6241 0625 (9 pm – 10 pm)
Mrs Jessie Phua   : 9745 1945 (9 am – 6 pm)
Mrs Maureen Aw : 9628 2069 (Mon – Sat; 8 am – 9 pm)
Mdm Sharon Tan : 9626 9409 (9 am – 10 pm)

Diploma and Degree Courses in Buddhism
Tertiary education in Buddhist Studies leading to award of Diploma, BA, MA and PhD degrees of the Buddhist & Pali University of Sri Lanka.
For enquiries, please contact:
Mdm Gina Tan : 9180 6505 (9 am – 5 pm)

Meditation Classes and Retreats
Regular meditation classes and quarterly retreats are being conducted by Ven. U Cittara. For information on latest schedule of dates & time, please refer to the website: **www.mangalavihara.org.sg**
For enquiries, please contact:
Bro. Sam Ho for registration : 9820 8050 or samhopru@yahoo.com.sg

Yoga Classes
Regular Beginners, Intermediate and Advanced level classes.
For enquiries, please contact:
Anthony Loy : 9001 9669 or visit www.yogaconnections.com.sg

Singapore Buddhist Mission – Youth Group

9 Ruby Lane Singapore 328284
Tel: 6299-7216
Website: www.sbmyouth.org   Email: sbm_youth@yahoo.com

Singapore Buddhist Mission (SBM) was initiated by the late Venerable Dr. K Sri Dhammananda Nayaka Thera and was established in November 1981.

The Youth Group of SBM was formed in 1996 and comprises of vibrant young Buddhists aged from 13 to 28. We aim to provide a fellowship for young people to come together and learn to walk the Buddha's path through various activities like sharing sessions, Dhamma talks, camps and music.

For more information, please visit our webpage at: www.sbmyouth.org

Saturday Sharing Sessions
The Youth Group gathers for a Dhamma sharing session every Saturday from 3.00pm to 6.00pm. There is also a short meditation session and movies are sometimes screened. All interested youths are welcome to join in.

Camp Ehi-Passiko
This is a Buddhist camp organized by the Youth Group and held since 1997. It takes place twice a year in June and December and serves to introduce Buddhism to young participants from the ages of 13 to 21. Programmes include games, singing sessions, interactive Dhamma sessions, Dhamma talks and campfires.

If you are interested to take part, please email us at :
sbm_youth@yahoo.com

Uttamayanmuni Buddhist Temple

32B, Hong San Terrace, Singapore 688785

Brief History

The temple is of the Thai Theravada Buddhist tradition and closely affiliated with the Kelantanese Thai Monastic Chapter (Khana song rat Kelantan) in Malaysia.

The temple was founded by Ven. Phra Vicaranayanmuni (Chao Khun Khron 1876 – 1962), former late Chief Abbot of Wat Uttamaram (aka Wat Bant Saet) in the village of Bang Saet, Pasir Mas, Kelantan. In 1962, Chao Khun Khron was invited to visit Singapore by his devotees here. During his visit, he informed his followers of his intention to build a temple in Singapore. Mr Tan Khe Wat, a devotee who was present during Chao Khun Khron visit, willingly offered a piece of land 2.5 ha in size to the Venerable for the construction of the temple. The temple was constructed in 1963 and was named Wat Uttamayanmuni and later Uttamayanmuni Buddhist Temple.

Objectives of the Temple are as follows:

(a) To propagate the teachings of the Buddha through lectures, discussions, activities, and publications;
(b) To encourage the teaching, practice and realisation of the Buddha's Dhamma-Vinaya;
(c) To support the Buddhist Monastic Order (Sangha), so they may act as spiritual guides and ministers for the well being of the Buddhist community;
(d) To promote harmony, tolerance and loyalty amongst Buddhists towards others and the nation; and
(e) To promote charitable, humanitarian and community causes and activities for the relief of pain and suffering of all living beings;

Our Regular Activities

Evening Chanting	07.30 pm – 08.30 pm
Sunday Morning Service and Puja	09.00 am – 11.00 am
Chinese Dhamma Course	
Monthly Weekend Meditation	

Our Annual Activities

New Year Offerings (Tak Bart) to Sangha	- January
Chinese New Year	- January / February
Magha Puja Day & Chap Gor Meh	- Full Moon Day of CNY
Ching Ming & Songkran Festival	- April
Vesak Day	- May
Memorial Service of Phor Than and May Chee	- May
Asalha Puja Day	- July
Ullambana	- August
Rap Pret (Ancestor Memorial Service)	- September (Full Moon)
Song Pret (Ancestor Memorial Service)	- September 30th
Kathina (Offering of Robes)	- November
Founder's Memorial Service	- November / December

Contact us:

enquiry@ uttamayanmuni.org
http://www.uttamayanmuni.org

Visuddha Meditation Centre

34 Bedok Walk S. 469135
(near to Tanah Merah MRT, opposite Palelai Buddhist Temple)
Bus no. 2, 9, 10 &14
Tel: 90101663

Myanmar - Pa Auk Sayadaw meditation method
Forest meditation technique

Free meditation course, course for beginners, meditation class.
Every Sunday of the month 1:30pm to 2:30pm. Total 4 lessons.
Tel : 90101663 (please SMS your name to register)

The meditation method taught in the centre is based on the instructions
as given in the Pali Tipitaka and Visuddhimagga, Seven Visuddhi, Sila,
Samadhi and Panna, beginning with Anapanassati or the four elements
to practice Samatha and Vipassana meditation.

The centre provides a conducive, free-of-charge and quiet place for
meditation. It opens daily from 7am to 9pm. There are "interview
sessions" both in the morning and evening to benefit those who are
busy working in the afternoon.

Weekend Retreat
"Saturday group meditation"
"Sunday group meditation"
(You are free to come for practice at anytime).

"**Course for Beginners**" Every Sat. and Sun. 9am to 7pm
(You are free to choose your own timing to join the course)

Ven. Visuddhacara   www.visuddha-m-c.org

*Free distribution booklets, VCDs and CDs are available in the centre
and through the website. Email: visuddha77@yahoo.com.sg*

Wat Ananda Metyarama Buddhist Temple

50-B Jalan Bukit Merah Singapore 169545
Bukit Merah Central Post Office P.O. Box No. 0603 Singapore 911534

Wat Ananda Youth - "Live the Dhamma"

Wat Ananda Youth (WAY) formerly known as the Ananda Metyarama Buddhist Youth Circle, was established in 1966.

Our Vision

To propagate the Dhamma through spiritual friendship and practice-focused interest groups.

Our Activities

Sunday Morning Service (SMS)

Speakers are invited to share on the Dhamma and how they apply it in their everyday life.
Date: Every Sunday
Time: 9.30am
Venue: Main Shrine

Bi-weekly Group meditation sessions:

Group sittings are held once every 2 weeks at the Wat Ananda Library.
Date: Every 2nd and 4th Sundays
Location: Wat Ananda Library
Time: 11.00am - 12.30pm

Vipassana Meditation

Date: Every Thursday (New classes start every 1st Thursday of the Month)
Time: 7.00pm - 9.00pm
Venue: Library

Ehipassiko Chanting Group - Warming the Heart, Freeing the Mind

The Ehipassiko Chanting Group (ECG) provides free Buddhist chanting services for wakes with the Wat Ananda Youth (WAY) as its custodian and in association with the Buddhist Fellowship. The objectives of ECG are: To practice and propagate the Dhamma through the proper ways of conducting a Buddhist funeral/wake service.

WAY Youth Networking for Professionals @ the City

The Youth Networking provides a platform for young working adults between 25 to 35 years old to network and learn about the Dhamma in the City area. It is usually held once a month on a Friday night.

Contact Us

Email: way1966@gmail.com
Website: http://www.way.org.sg/

THEKCHEN CHOLING (SINGAPORE)
2 Beatty Lane, Singapore 209945
Tel: +6564663720, Fax: +6564656736
Website: www.thekchencholing.org
Email: administrator@thekchencholing.org

Singapore-born Lama Thubten Namdrol Dorje founded TCCL in 2001 as instructed by his late teacher H.E. Geshe Lama Konchog, who has reincarnated as Lama Phuntsok Rinpoche of Kopan Monastery, Nepal.

Although we are of the Gelug tradition of Tibetan Buddhism, we practise non-sectarianism, embracing all schools of Buddhism as a reminder of how Lord Shakyamuni Buddha's compassion and skillful means reach out to all beings through his 84,000 teachings. As such, Lama Dorje strongly advocates all students to have a strong foundation and understanding of Theravada teachings and practices even as they embark on the Mahayana path.

Through regular weekly teachings in English and Mandarin, chanting, prayer sessions and other events, our resident nuns and lay students receive a well-rounded understanding and experience of Buddhism, realizing how the application of the Dharma can make a real difference in their daily lives and as a result be of benefit to all.

In order to realize one of our objectives to be an easily accessible place of refuge at all times of the day or night, we are the first Tibetan Buddhist temple in Singapore to open 24 hours a day, 7 days a week. The main hall is available to all who seek a place of quiet, for prayers or meditation at any time of the day.

As a healing centre, we provide free TCM medical consulting service, acupuncture service and medicine twice a week in the temple. Our social outreach program includes free medicine distribution, free meals and finance support, with emphasis for the poor and elderly.

We have been granted permission by the Office of HH the 14th Dalai Lama to publish his books in simplified Mandarin for free distribution. Besides this, we publish and distribute sutras and other Dharma books too.

Metta Welfare Association

Founded in 1992 by Venerable Shi Fa Zhao and registered as a charity in 1994, Metta Welfare Association (Metta) provides quality health care and welfare services to the needy regardless of race or religion through our nine centres segregated into the Disability, Medical and Community Care, Special Education and Social Enterprise. From the young to the elderly, the infirmed to the terminally ill, we offer a wide range of services that go beyond the mere fulfillment of their needs.

Endorsed by the Ministry of Community Development, Youth and Sports, Ministry of Health and Ministry of Education, we are also a member of the National Council of Social Service, Singapore Hospice Council and Singapore Disability Sports Council.

For donations and queries, please contact :

Metta Welfare Association
32 Simei Street 1, Metta Building
Singapore 529950
Tel: (65) 65804688
Fax: (65) 65804699

E-mail: events@metta.org.sg
Website: www.metta.org.sg

The printing of 100,000 copies of this booklet has been made possible through the generosity of the following. May the Blessings of the Triple Gem be with them always.

Ehipassiko Chanting Group (ECG)
Firefly Mission

The Bay family
The Lee family

Mr. Thomas Goh
Mr. Wong Hong Kian
Mr. Jeffrey Tan Kok Siong

To share in the merits of reprinting or distributing this and other Dhamma books, please contact us for more details :

KepMedia International Pte Ltd
22 Jurong Port Road Tower A #04-01
Singapore 619114
Tel: 6896 0030 Fax: 6896 0070
Email: leeshin@kepmedia.com.sg
or :
www.justbegood.net
Email: admin@justbegood.net

The Gift of the Dhamma is the greatest Gift of all

The significance of sharing the Dhamma

When you share the Dhamma, others will also share the Dhamma with you in your future lives. This is the principle of kamma.

Because the Dhamma can only be shared in the human and heavenly realms, you must be reborn in either of these realms for others to share the Dhamma with you.

Thus, by sharing the Dhamma, you not only give the greatest gift of all, you also help to ensure favourable rebirths for yourself.

More importantly, sharing the Dhamma leads to peace and happiness and eventually to Nibbana, for both the giver and the receiver.

These are the reasons why the gift of the Dhamma is the greatest gift of all.

A daily aspiration

May I always do my best to help protect and spread the teachings of the Buddha for the benefit of all beings;

And may I always continue to learn and practice the true Dhamma until I attain Nibbana.

T Y Lee